MW01244007

Shushan's
Shenanigans

ii

Parker's Poetry Plus Inc. First Edition 2018
Copyright © 2020 by Joel B. Parker
Published in the U.S.A. by:
Parker's Poetry Plus Inc. Brooklyn, NY
Poetically Correct Short Story Collection; Vol. I
Written solely by: Joel B. Parker
AKA – The ≠ Poet Joel
Cover Design by: Dexter Koonce
MSFA 25th Anniversary Special Edition

ISBN-13: 978-1-72264-996-6
Printed in the United States of America
www. ParkersPoetryPlus.com

This book is dedicated to:

My First Sunday School Teachers:

My Mother, the late Cora M. Parker
My Aunt, the late Elease Kellum
My Maternal Grandfather, The Late Grover Ballard
Sunday School Superintendent
My First Pastor, the late Dr. Walter L. Harding Sr.
Deacon Howard Edlow
Dr. Jeanette Edlow
All of the above from the St. Luke Baptist Church
Located at: 103 Morningside Ave, NY, NY 10027

TABLE OF CONTENTS

Chapter   Pg.#

TABLE OF CONTENTS

Chapter   Pg.#

PREFACE

This is the entire ten chapters of the book of Esther. This and Ruth are only two books of the Bible written in honor of, and entitled with the name of a woman. Surprisingly, this is the only book of the Bible that doesn't mention God.

The Book of Esther relates the story of a Hebrew woman in Persia, born as Hadassah but known as Esther. In Biblical Names the meaning of the name Esther is: **Secret, hidden**. This is an intriguing story of mass deception, mass partying and mass survival. Under the tutelage of her cousin Mordecai, Esther hid her Jewish heritage long enough to impress the King Xerxes to make her the Queen. The previous Queen, Vashti lost her position and ultimately her life because she openly embarrassed the king by refusing to present herself at his command. To find a replacement they held a beauty contest and Esther won.

The antagonist, villain in this story was a man named Haman who sought to annihilate all the Jews; history shows, a pogrom commonly known as genocide is not new. Haman known as "Haman the Agagite" or "Haman the evil", manipulated the King into initially agreeing with his homicidal plan. However, using this verbiage which became a famous quote: Esther proclaimed the following: "If I Perish, I perish", and she went to see the King. Despite the fact that coming before the king without being summoned and or permission was cause for execution. Esther had the eye of the king, and now she had his ear. While in his presence she revealed her lineage, appealed to the favor she had with the king, and exposed the plot Haman which concocted. The King heard her plea and changed his decree sparing Jews in all of the one hundred, twenty-seven (127) provinces which he ruled over. It's interesting because women in general didn't have outwardly prominent roles, but in this story a woman is a hero who was instrumental in saving an entire culture.

As a result of being spared, the Jews to this day have a celebration called Purim. It is celebrated by: **Exchanging gifts of food and drink known as mishloach manot**. ... Eating a celebratory meal known as a se'udat Purim. Public recitation ("reading of the megillah") of the Scroll of Esther, known as kriat ha-megillah, usually in synagogue. The ironic traditional dessert is a "Hamantashen" cookie. It is a fruit-filled, shortbread pastry named after Haman. It is shaped like the hat Haman wore and symbolizes how he crumbled.

This is the Poetically Correct Short Story entitled:
Shushan's Shenanigans, written by: **The ≠ Poet Joel.**

ACKNOWLEGEMENTS

The entire Young Israel Jewish Temple of Holliswood. The nicest collective group of people, I have ever encountered, at any Synagogue. Special recognition to Rabbi Moshe Taub, Keith Landsman, Ira Kreisler, Murray (Rockin' Roll Johnny) Bod, Jason Chernikoff, Yakir & Mira (baseball mom) Wockstock, James O'Connell, Kevi & Chani Neuman. My favorite newlyweds: Shelly & Marlene Schwartz. Even the Children: Hadassah Taub, Sam & Abigail Chernikof, who make it a point to greet me every week. Thank you for accepting, embracing and not just tolerating, but befriending an African American Christian. A reminder that there is still hope for this world. Last but not least, My entire Morning Star Fellowship Assemblies family, for your constant support. Especially on this 25th Silver Anniversary under the leadership of:

Bishop Dwight P. Dove, Presider

Bishop Darrell K. Dove Sr., Vice Presider

Bishop Samuel Bacon, Chairman Board of Bishops

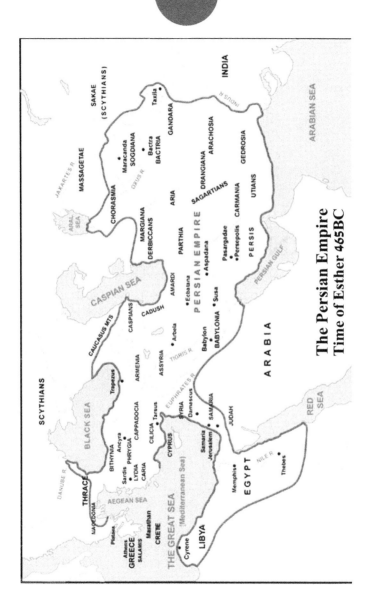

The Persian Empire
Time of Esther 465BC

WARNING:

This book may cause you to be bold, take more risks and definitely trust your spiritual advisors and God.

Chapter 1 - 10
Poetically

The book of Esther from the scrolls of Megillah begins
with a portion of scripture, with a very common phrase
written 1204 times "wayehi" in the Hebrew Bible
but only 453 in the standard Christian King James

It introduces us to a King Ahasuerus, also known as Xerxes
from India even unto Ethiopia was his span
he reigned over one hundred, twenty-seven (127) provinces
but he lodged in his palace, in Shushan

Founded by King Darius
completed by king Artaxerus
of the Kings of Persia
he is noted as the richest

The Elamites, Persian & Parthian empire,
it was their principle city
Shushan by definition means Lily
It was once flourishing and very pretty

In Esther, and once in both Nehemiah and Daniel
These are the only books you see reference of Shushan
Located About 150 miles north of the Persian Gulf
Today it would be Western Iran

Nevertheless, as the story goes
The King Ahasuerus in the 3rd year of his reign
Made a feast unto his princes and servants
Showing his riches for 180 days, boastful and vain

Afterwards in the palace courtyard
he made another 7-day feast
This was for all the people in Shushan
From the greatest to the least

there were white, green, and blue hangings,
fastened with cords of fine linen
and purple to silver rings and pillars of marble
solid no fake fill in

the beds were of gold and silver,
upon a pavement of red, and blue, and white, and black marble
they gave drink in diverse vessels of gold;
the royal wine was in abundance and plentiful

instructions were given to the palace officers
and at the king's command
they should fulfil the pleasures
of every single man

"Also, Vashti the queen made a feast
"For the women in the royal house
which belonged to Ahasuerus"
this was separate from her king and spouse

"On the 7th day, when the heart of the king
was merry with wine, he commanded
Mehuman, Biztha, Harbona, Bigtha, & Abagtha, Zethar,
& Carcas," who did as demanded

They were "the 7 chamberlains
that served in the presence of the king,"
They were ordered
"To bring -

Vashti the queen before the king
with the crown royal,"
"To shew the people and the princes her beauty: for she was
fair to look on" But his posturing plan, queen Vashti did spoil

All that celebration and merriment
Was flipped in one moment of one night
You don't have to be royal, or a rocket scientist
To see the severity of this plight

Vashti the queen, blatantly refused
Ahasuerus the king's commandment
She didn't do it in private, rather in public
In front of the king's most trusted and powerful cabinet

"The king was very wroth.
And his anger burned within him."
After all this was done in front of guests
Honestly, This had to be very embarrassing

"Then the King said
to the wise men"
all that knew law and judgement
seeking the protocol for this egregious sin

"And the next unto him was
Carshena, Shethar, Admatha, Tarshish, Mere,
Marsena, and Memucan". which first in the Kingdom
All being some of the most prominent men there

These were "the seven (7) princes of Persia and Media
which saw the king's face"
They all concurred that this act of defiance
Was an outright unacceptable disgrace.

They continued saying this wrong was done to all
the princes, and all the people, oh king, not only to you
realistically they couldn't unsee what they,
nor what was done could they undo

As word spreads and this contempt, is reported to all the
provinces; For what she did in public cannot be hid
it will give occasion and fuel for all wives
to possibly do as she did

"Thus shall there arise
too much contempt and wrath"
the handwriting on the wall
it's simple math

"If it please the king,
let there go a royal commandment from him,
and let it be written among the laws of
the Persians and the Medes," send it to all of them

so it is known throughout the land and let it not be altered,
Vashti can no longer come before the king Ahasuerus;
"give her royal estate unto another that is better than she"
As King, that was both lawful and just

That decree was published in every language throughout all his
empire, and those words to the king sounded really good
It gave the princes some comfort and empowerment. Even
the common could say with royal authority "I wish my wife would"

With that settled the king's anger was kindled, knowing
what was decreed against Vashti, his wrath appeased
Now the servants had the arduous task
of finding a virgin with whom the king would be pleased

So, the word went out in all the provinces
to the keeper of the women
that the preliminary search for all the fair young virgins
should immediately begin

They gathered them unto Shushan Palace under the custody
of Hege the king's chamberlain and preparation commenced
Oil of myrrh, spices and ointments
for purification were dispensed

it was proposed the maiden
which pleased the king
would be queen instead of Vashti
and he eagerly agreed with that thing

It's amazing how calculated and precise God is,
not operating in coincidences and happenstance.
How he is deliberate in orchestrating
Not leaving anything to chance

I am compelled to take this moment, to illuminate
to most and reveal to some a very subjective view
Esther 2:5 states:
"Now in Shushan the Palace there was a certain Jew,"

"whose name was Mordecai,"
A name meaning warrior in Hebrew
the specificity, certainty and lineage at his mention
done like only a God who fore knew

He was "the son of Jair, the son of Shimei,
the son of Kish, a Benjamite;"
Who had been carried away from Jerusalem with the
captivity" Jeremiah 22, the Prophesied of this plight

"Which had been carried away with Jeconiah
king of Judah," (AKA) Coniah and also as Jehoiachin
he was the grandson of Josiah,
and son of Jehoiakim

Whom Nebuchadnezzar
the king of Babylon had carried away"
But it's beginning to look like the integral parts
Of a foundation for a new day

Shushan's Shenanigans - By Joel B. Parker

Although Mordecai was prominently positioned
His role was to facilitate
A lesson to learn; we must all learn our place
In doing so we can still be noticed and great

It appears he was the stabilizer for the main character
for whom this book was named
He raised Hadassah, Hebrew for who we know as Esther;
Let's embark on that which brought them both fame

Esther was the daughter of Mordecai's uncle's Abihail,
after both her parents died, he took her as his own daughter.
and in answer to the search and decree, to the custody of
Hegai, keeper of the women is where he brought her

at first look, she was noted
as a favorable candidate
and Hegai speedily gave Esther her things for purification
he became somewhat of an advocate

In addition to the perfumes and ointments was
a preferred place in the palace to stay
and seven personal maidens
Esther was already on a subliminal display

six months with oil and Myrrh, then six months with sweet
odours the entire purification process was 12 months long
Mordecai, walked by the court of the women's house
Everyday monitoring, to see if anything had gone wrong

The time had finally come,
every maiden was brought before the king
and were given the opportunity to bring items of their choice
But Esther desired no special thing

"In the evening she went,
And on the morrow she returned
Into the second house of the women"
Where she sojourned

Now from Hegai's care to the second house; the keeper of
the concubines, Shaashgaz another of the king's chamberlain
Where she would come in to the king no more
Except if the king delighted in her and called her by name

As expected Esther obtained favour in the sight of them all
Thus, she was taken unto King Ahasuerus and into his house
In the tenth month "Tebeth" in the seventh year of his reign
He made Esther Queen and his new spouse

Shushan's Shenanigans - By Joel B. Parker

She replaced Vashti,
and now wore the Royal Crown
And the King loved Esther above all women,
for she was pleasing. She won hands down

"Then the king made a great feast
unto all his princes and servants "even Esther's feast;"
"and gave gifts according to the state of the king"
to all the provinces, he made a release

"And when the virgins were gathered together
the second time, then Mordecai
sat in the king's gate"
and what he witnessed, most it would mortify

This whole time, Esther didn't reveal her kindred
Mordecai, charged her to keep it hidden
A Jew in the king's inner court, I would liken to a black slave
Married to a white U.S. President; In any era, still forbidden

However, the king had two eunuchs, Bigthan and Teresh
In the king's gate, they kept the door
But they were wroth, desiring to lay hands on the king,
In a manner that the king would live no more

Mordecai who sat in the gate,
now aware of the plot and knowing this was not a game
He told Esther, who in turn told the king
However, she certified it in Mordecai's name

Therefore, was an inquisition made
of the matter
after all they couldn't just take the word of a Jew
especially if it were just second hand chatter

After intense questioning,
it was found to be true.
Both Bigthan and Teresh were hanged on a tree
It is recorded in the book of Chronicles of those two

After these things the king Ahasuerus took Haman
The son of Hammedatha the Agagite and promoted him
At the king's command all reverenced and bowed
As far as the princes, his seat was above all of them

"And all the king's servants,
 that were in the king's gate, bowed
and reverenced Haman: for the king had so commanded
concerning him." They were overwhelmingly wowed

However, Mordecai refused to bow
For Haman he reverenced not
The king's servants asked Mordecai why he transgressed the
kings commandment and they then put Haman on the spot

They told Haman and he was so frustrated with Mordecai
but mindful of the multitude, he didn't know what to do
In a rage, throwing a tantrum
He conspired to kill Mordecai, and also every single Jew

Haman was so full of pompous pride,
wrath and indignation
he began to orchestrate a genocidal plot
He planned to kill not just one man but a whole nation

"In the first month, that is, the month Nisan,
in the twelfth year of king Ahasuerus,
they cast Pur, that is, the lot, before Haman from day to day,"
in chance they did believe and trust

"and from month to month, to the twelfth month,
that is, the month Adar." They drew straws
Yes, every day, every month 'til the 12th month
Every matter was left up to a lucky draw

"And Haman said unto king Ahasuerus,
There is a certain people scattered abroad and dispersed
among the people in all the provinces of thy kingdom;
and their laws are diverse

from all people;
neither keep they the king's laws:
therefore it is not for the king's profit to suffer them."
They have just too many flaws

"If it please the king,
let it be written
that they may be destroyed:"
Haman proposed that they all be smitten

Shushan's Shenanigans - By Joel B. Parker

"and I will pay ten thousand talents of silver to
the hands of those that have the charge of the business,
to bring *it* into the king's treasuries."
Unfortunately that made lucrative sense.

That value would be approximately three billion dollars
according to a 2018 money scale exchange
the king took his ring off his hand, gave it to Haman
and didn't care or think anything was strange

"Then were the King's scribes called on
and they wrote, in the 1st month on the 13th day
unto all the King's lieutenants, governors and rulers
of every people in every province, what Haman had to say

the letters were sent by posts
sealed with the King's ring
with a date; the 13th day of the 12th month Adar
in that one day they were to enforce this thing

which was "to destroy, to kill, and to cause to perish all Jews,
both young and old, little children and women," what next?
"And the King and Haman sat down to drink;
but the city Shushan was perplexed."

"When Mordecai perceived all that was done.
Mordecai rent his clothes, and put on sackcloth and ashes,
and went out into the midst of the city, and cried
with a loud and bitter cry;" as if he received physical lashes

"When Mordecai perceived all that was done"
He rent his clothes, and wailed with loud bitter cries
Wearing sackcloth and ashes, outside the King's gate
He was a sight for sore eyes

Wearing sackcloth and ashes,
outside the King's gate
clearly he wasn't presentable
and in no position to facilitate

"For none might enter into the King's gate clothed with
sackcloth." Queen Esther at the news was also grieved
She sent clean raiment to clothe Mordecai
But those garments he would not receive

In every province where this decree was published
The Jews were fasting, mourning and weeping
It was at this time Mordecai called on Esther
To reveal the secret, she was keeping

Shushan's Shenanigans - By Joel B. Parker

In depth, he wanted her to go in unto the King
Making supplication, which is a humble, earnest request
Pleading for him to spare her people (the Jews), Knowing
anyone coming to the king on their own could be put to death

To come to the inner court before the king,
for any man or woman, the ritualistic procedure was clear,
he summoned you, or either he'd find favor
hold out the golden scepter, then your petition he'd hear

Esther corresponded back and forth with Mordecai
through "Hatach" one of the king's chamberlains
Esther's contention was that she was not summoned now
and hadn't been for the past thirty days.

Mordecai stressed the urgency of this imposition
Noting the importance and need for selflessness
Adding,   **who knoweth whether thou art
come to the kingdom for such a time as this"**

Highlighting, that she herself was a Jew
Her and her father's house might not be spared
Without some intervention; if she held her peace
of that fate one should be prepared

After careful consideration,
She came to the obvious conclusion
Her escaping destruction
Was just another illusion

So, she solicited prayer from Mordecai
Asking for 3 days and nights, all the Jews in Shushan to fast
Consenting to do that which is not according to the law
Saying "if I perish, I perish" that petition she was going to ask

"So Mordecai
went his way,
and did according to all that Esther had commanded him."
Which was simply to tell all the Jews to fast and pray

"Now it came to pass on the 3rd day that Esther put on
her royal apparel and stood in the inner court
of the King's house," and as the king sat on his throne
His attention Esther caught

He held out the golden scepter
As she so desperately desired
The king asked her what her request was
And he seemed excited, as he inquired

So much so he told her
before she could even ask
Whatever she wanted would be granted unto her
even the kingdom she could have up to half

With poise and wisdom
she took it slow asking him
If the king along with Haman this day
would attend a banquet she prepared for them?

"Then the king said, Cause Haman to make haste,
that he may do as Esther hath said.
So the King and Haman came to the banquet"
and verse 6 said it was wine that they were fed

And the king said unto Esther
"what is thy petition?"
She asked that they would on tomorrow
Another banquet attend,

That first banquet must have really been nice
cause Haman's day was joyful, and his heart was glad,
but when he saw Mordecai in the King's gate
showing him no regard, again he got mad

Against Mordecai,
Haman was full of indignation
but he refrained himself and went home
to brag to his family about his invitation

For, besides the king
he was the only one
that was present at Esther's banquet
he continued to boast of all that was done

how he was promoted and advanced
above the princes and servants of the king
but seeing Mordecai the Jew in the king's court
all that honor seemed to not mean a thing

"then said Zeresh his wife and all his friends
Let the gallows be made of fifty cubits high
And on to morrow speak thou unto the king that
Mordecai be hanged thereon:"(they all wanted him to die)

She continued saying "then go thou in merrily
With the king unto the banquet.
And the thing pleased Haman;
And he caused the gallows to be made. (the plan was now set)

"On that night could not the king sleep, and he commanded
to bring the book of records of the chronicles;
and they were read before the king." in his hearing
There were pleasant, motivational, audibles

For they read of the conspiracy of Bigthana and Teresh
to kill the king, which Mordecai thwarted
and he now wanted to know what honor and dignity
was bestowed, but Mordecai had not been rewarded

the servants confirmed that nothing was done for him
then the king asked who was outside his house, in the court
they answered, it was Haman coming to speak to the king
and it was Mordecai's hanging which he sought

the king said unto his servants
let him come in
the dialogue that follows
gets very interesting

the king asked Haman,
"What shall be done
unto the man whom the king delighted to honour?
Haman in his vanity thought he was the one

Shushan's Shenanigans - By Joel B. Parker

"Now Haman thought in his heart,
To whom would the king delight to do honour
more than to myself"
his speech now matched his entitled persona

Haman replied: Let the royal apparel the king would wear,
the horse on which the king rides
and the royal crown on his head. And it be delivered by
a noble prince in whom the king confides

And with these things, he should be arrayed
And that he be brought on horseback
through the street of the city and him proclaim
the king replied "make haste" wanting no slack

what a rude awakening to find out,
as far as being honored, not only that he wasn't the one
but he was assigned to personally deliver
and get this bittersweet job done

then said the King, let nothing fail
of all that thou hast spoken,
I could imagine the thoughts of Haman
Probably saying "you've got to be jokin'

Nevertheless, Haman took the horse
The royal apparel too
and as the king commanded
delivered them to Mordecai the Jew

Haman with his head covered
he began to mourn
although he paraded him through the city
Mordecai, he continued to scorn

He went home venting
to Zeresh, his wife
and to all of his friends
how things were going wrong in his life

Then said his wise men and Zeresh
after listening to it all
If Mordecai be of the seed of the Jews
thou will not prevail, but before him fall

"And while they
were yet talking with him,
came the King's chamberlains and hasted to bring Haman"
unto the banquet that Esther had prepared." for them

"So the King and Haman came to the banquet with Esther"
And said unto Esther "on the 2ⁿᵈ day at the banquet of wine
What is thy petition," and "what is thy request?"
Up to half my kingdom, it shall be thine

"Then queen Esther answered and said"
As she finally divulged her heart
"If I have found favour in thy sight, oh king,"
With that humble spirit is how she chose to start

"if I please the King,
Let my life be given me
at my petition, and my people at my request"
our plight you need to see

"For we are sold, I and my people,
to be destroyed, to be slain,
and to perish" sold for bondmen and bond women
Manipulatively mocking the King's reign

"I had held my tongue,
although the enemy could not"
He used the king's power and authority
to execute his own personal plot

"Then the King Ahasuerus answered and said"
In an angry tone, really wanting to know
"who is he, and where is he,
That durst presume in his heart to do so?"

"And Esther said,
The adversary"
is the wicked Haman
He is the enemy

"Then Haman was afraid before the king and queen.
And the King arising from the banquet of wine in his wrath
went into the palace garden" gee what was he thinking?
Hmmm, King is angry, enemy exposed; you do the math

"and Haman stood up to make request
for his life to Esther the queen;
for he saw that there was evil determined against him
by the king". But that's what you get when you're mean

"then the King returned out of the palace garden
into the place of the banquet wine;
and Haman was fallen upon the bed whereon Esther was."
To an onlooker, it would appear that Haman lost his mind.

"Then said the king,
will he force the queen also before me in the house?"
they covered Haman's face
As the word went out of the King's mouth

"And Harbonah, one of the chamberlains, said before
the King, Behold also, the gallows fifty cubits high,
which Haman had made
for Mordecai,"

"who had spoken good for the King"
The King, now wanting this wrong rectified
ordered Haman hung on the gallows prepared for Mordecai
"Then was the King's wrath pacified"

"On that day did the King Ahasuerus
give the house of Haman the Jews' enemy
unto Esther the queen" which she in turn gave to Mordecai
Oh, what sweet irony

" And Mordecai came before the king;
for Esther told what he was to her" how they were related
The King took off his ring which he took from Haman
gave it to Mordecai; he was instantly elevated

"And Esther spake yet again before the King,
and fell down at his feet,
and besought him with tears"
for there was more condition she needed him to meet

She asked the king "to put away the mischief
of Haman the Agagite,
and his device that he had devised against the Jews."
so much wrong needed to be made right

"then the King held out the golden scepter toward Esther.
So Esther arose, and stood before the King. And said"
"let it be written to the reverse the letters
which Haman sent out, with authority before he was dead.

Shushan's Shenanigans - By Joel B. Parker

Haman the son of Hammedatha the Agagite
Wrote to all the King's provinces, to destroy all the Jews
"How can I endure to see the evil that shall come unto my
people?" -She needed to bring her people uplifting news

"Then King Ahasuerus said unto Esther the queen
and to Mordecai the Jew, " the following news
"Behold, I have given Esther the house of Haman, and him
they have hanged," because he laid hands on the Jews

"Write ye also for the Jews, as it liketh you,
in the King's name, and seal it with the King's ring;
for the writing, which is written in the King's name, and
sealed with the King's ring," No man can reverse that thing

"Then were the King's scribes called at that time
in the third month, that is, the month Sivan
on the three and twentieth day thereof,"
were new letters of authority given

"and it was written according to all that Mordecai
commanded" to the lieutenants, and the deputies
unto the Jews," which spanned
the Black, Caspian, Arabian, Red, and the Great seas

That's all the rulers of the provinces
"which are from India to Ethiopia,"
all the devastation Haman initially initiated,
was now turned from annihilation to a virtual utopia

127 provinces each in their own languages "and to the
Jews according to their writing" and understanding
"And he wrote in King Ahasuerus' name,
And sealed it with the King's ring" - outstanding

"and sent letters by posts on horseback, and riders on mules,
camels and young dromedaries
the king granted rights to the Jews in every city
to defend themselves against their adversaries

to not only defend, but to stand for their lives
to cause to perish, to destroy, to slay
all "that would assault them, both little ones and women,
and to take the spoil of them for a prey"

"upon the thirteenth day of the twelfth month
which is the month Adar"
the copy of the King's commandment was published
unto all people, near and far

Shushan's Shenanigans - By Joel B. Parker

"And the decree was given
at Shushan palace.
And Mordecai went out from the presence of the king"
without any more malice

clothed "in royal apparel of blue and white
and with a great crown of gold,
and with a garment of fine linen and purple;"
in with the new, away with the old

"and the city of Shushan rejoiced and was glad,
"the Jews had light, and gladness,
and joy and honour. And in every province, and in every
city,"- amongst the Jews, there was no more sadness

"whithersoever the king's commandment
and decree came,
the Jews had joy and gladness,
a feast and a good day", for they overcame

"and many of the people
of the land
became Jews, for the fear of the Jews fell upon them"
who now had the upper hand

"Now in the twelfth month, that is, the month Adar,
On the thirteenth day of the same
When the King's commandment and his decree drew near
To be put in execution," there was a new acclaim

"in the day that the enemies of the Jews
Hoped to have power over them,
(though it was turned to the contrary,
That the Jews had rule over them that hated them;)"

"The Jews gathered themselves together in their cities
throughout all the provinces of the King Ahasuerus,
to lay hand on such as sought their hurt:
and no man could withstand them;" I can picture the ruckus

"for the fear of them fell on the people.
And all the rulers of the provinces, and the lieutenants,
and the deputies, and officers of the King, helped the Jews,
because the fear of Mordecai;" Sweet recompense.

"For Mordecai was great in the King's house,
and his fame went out throughout
all the provinces: for this man Mordecai
waxed greater and greater." He now had real clout

Shushan's Shenanigans - By Joel B. Parker

"Thus the Jews smote all their enemies
with the stroke of the sword, and slaughter, and destruction,
and did what they would unto those that hated them."
That's what you call, mass enemy reduction

"And in Shushan the palace
the Jews slew and destroyed five hundred men."
Including but not limited to
The ten sons of Haman

For the record those ten sons were, "Parshandatha,
and Dalphon, and Aspatha, And Poratha,
and Adalia and Aridatha, And Parmashta,
and Arisai, and Aridai, and Vajezatha"

After all these events were told to the King,
he asked Esther if there was anything further to be done?
She requested on to morrow that there be a hanging
on the gallows of Haman's ten sons.

"And the king commanded it
so to be done:
and the decree was given at Shushan;
and they hanged Haman's ten sons."

In total over seventy-five thousand
enemies of the Jews were slain
on the fourteenth and fifteenth of the month Adar
the Jews feasted and rested from their previous pain

and Mordecai wrote to all the Jews
and to all the provinces were these letters sent
that the fourteenth and fifteenth day of the month Adar
should be an annually celebrated event

and so, it was established
and accepted amongst all of them
because they did cast lots
it shall be called Purim

which includes reading the story
and a self-imposed fast of Esther
feasting and sending portions to one another
giving gifts to the poor and commemorating the ancestors

"And that these days should be remembered and kept
Throughout every generation, every family, every province,
and every city; and that these days of Purim should noy fail
from among the Jews, - it has continued ever since

"And the King Ahasuerus laid a tribute
upon the land, and upon the sea." - An emotional high
"And all the acts of his power and of his might, and the
declaration of the greatness of Mordecai,"

"whereunto the King advanced him, are they not written
in the book of chronicles of the kings of Media and Persia?"
"For Mordecai the Jew was next unto the king Ahasuerus,
and great among the Jews," - what a powerful merger.

Mordecai assumed the prominent position of authority
and by the King was glorified.
But we must take note and recognize, Esther who took the
risk, petitioning the King, for which she could have died

 "Pur 4 the course", as Hadassah the Heroine
was Trading Places, with the debunk, Vashti the queen
There was "A Lot, A Lady", with Mordecai praying
against one who is remembered as hamantashen

This Victorious Virgin, known to us as Esther served libation
infiltrated the Masqueraded, deception without panicking
went "From Annihilation to Saving a Nation"
exposing the charades of "Shushan's Shenanigans"

THE END

Parker's Poetic Puzzles
SCRAMBLE followed by WORD SEARCH
The Bible Book of: ESTHER Chapter 1

The following is not meant
to confuse or stump you
in fact to help
I will give you a clue

All the words in this puzzle are in the
1st chapter of Esther, so have fun
Using the Kings James Bible
The exact verse number is next to each one

After you unscramble the ten words
on the following page
Use the letters that have numbers under them
To reveal the below poetic phrase

				1	2	3	4		5	6	7	8	9	10	11	12			

				13	14	15		16	17	18		19	20	21	22	23	24			

Shushan's Shenanigans - By Joel B. Parker

	01.	02.	03.	04.	05.	06.	07.	08.	09.	10.	vs		01.	02.	03.	04.	05.	06.	07.	08.	09.	10.
01	E	C	V	R	P	S	O	I	N		1	01										■
																	7			16	3	
02	O	I	K	M	N	D	G				2	02								■	■	■
																2		12	17			
03	E	O	R	P	W						3	03							■	■	■	■
															8	18						
04	U	R	O	O	I	G	S	L			4	04									■	■
																	21	9		1	14	
05	D	A	A	E	U	N	B	C	N		7	05										■
																13		24			4	
06	A	B	U	Y	E	T					11	06							■	■	■	■
																5		15				
07	O	G	T	B	H	R	U				17	07								■	■	■
															22				7			
08	S	E	I	L	K	I	E	W			18	08									■	■
																	11			23		
09	D	H	S	S	N	A	B	U			20	09									■	■
																	6	19				
10	E	P	D	A	E	S	L				21	10								■	■	■
																5		20				
	01.	02.	03.	04.	05.	06.	07.	08.	09.	10.	vs		01.	02.	03.	04.	05.	06.	07.	08.	09.	10.

Chapters 1-10 _ Poetically – By: The ≠ Poet Joel

ABAGTHA	ADALIA	ADAR	ADMATHA
AHASUERUS	ARIDAI	ARIDATHA	ARISAI
ASPATHA	BIGTHA	BIZTHA	CARCAS
CARSHENA	DALPHON	ESTHER	ETHIOPIA
HADASSAH	HAMAN	HARBONA	HEGAI
JAIR	JECONIAH	JEWS	JUDAH
KISH	MARSENA	MEDIA	MEMUCAN
MERES	MORDECAI	PARMASHTA	PERSIA
PORATHA	SHETHAR	SHIMEI	SHUSHAN
TERESH	VASHTI	WINE	ZETHAR

After you find all forty words on the following page
Use the unused letters to reveal the below poetic phrase

They're already written in order So no need to fear
But to the directions you must adhere

It's relatively easy but take note this time
All the words used are in chapters on, two and nine

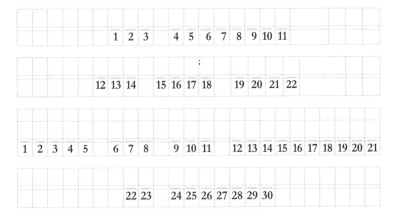

Parker's Poetic Puzzles
"WORD SEARCH"

Esther Chapters 1, 2, & 9

```
G A N E S R A M O B V S E R E M M
P A R M A S H T A I A W I N E D E
T H W A H D A R T G S E J E W S M
D O N I T A S H E T H A R E M A N
A S J D A L P L A H T A P S A A N
D T U E R P S H H A I N O C E J A
A A D M O H U A A R I S A I E S N
R N A E P O R H H M O R D E C A I
E O H A R N E T S R E A I L A D A
T B I A E I U A I N A H S U H S A
H R A B H E S D K T A H A M A N N
I A G A T M A I H D A I S R E P E
O H E G S I H R M H A D A S S A H
P T H T E H A A E D B I Z T H A S
I E C H H S T A I T E R E S H R R
A Z A A C H T R E R S R I A J I A
N S H U A S A H S A C R A C A N C
```

THE END

Well the end of the Poetic Story version,
But there is still more.
The literal text in English and Hebrew
I encourage you to explore

For your convenience, I know you have a bible
somewhere, but so you won't have to look
I included the entire ten chapters of Esther
Right inside this book

SHUSHAN'S SHENANIGANS

The book of Esther, written in Scriptural text in both Hebrew and English

Esther Chapter 1 אֶסְתֵּר

א וַיְהִי, בִּימֵי אֲחַשְׁוֵרוֹשׁ : הוּא אֲחַשְׁוֵרוֹשׁ, הַמֹּלֵךְ מֵהֹדּוּ וְעַד-כּוּשׁ--שֶׁבַע וְעֶשְׂרִים וּמֵאָה, מְדִינָה.

1 Now it came to pass in the days of Ahasuerus--this is Ahasuerus who reigned, from India even unto Ethiopia, over a hundred and seven and twenty provinces--

ב בַּיָּמִים, הָהֵם--כְּשֶׁבֶת הַמֶּלֶךְ אֲחַשְׁוֵרוֹשׁ, עַל כִּסֵּא מַלְכוּתוֹ, אֲשֶׁר, בְּשׁוּשַׁן הַבִּירָה.

2 that in those days, when the king Ahasuerus sat on the throne of his kingdom, which was in Shushan the castle,

ג בִּשְׁנַת שָׁלוֹשׁ, לְמָלְכוֹ, עָשָׂה מִשְׁתֶּה, לְכָל-שָׂרָיו וַעֲבָדָיו : חֵיל פָּרַס וּמָדַי, הַפַּרְתְּמִים וְשָׂרֵי הַמְּדִינוֹת--לְפָנָיו.

3 in the third year of his reign, he made a feast unto all his princes and his servants; the army of Persia and Media, the nobles and princes of the provinces, being before him;

ד בְּהַרְאֹתוֹ, אֶת-עֹשֶׁר כְּבוֹד מַלְכוּתוֹ, וְאֶת-יְקָר, תִּפְאֶרֶת גְּדוּלָּתוֹ ; יָמִים רַבִּים, שְׁמוֹנִים וּמְאַת יוֹם.

4 when he showed the riches of his glorious kingdom and the honour of his excellent majesty, many days, even a hundred and fourscore days.

ה וּבִמְלוֹאת הַיָּמִים
הָאֵלֶּה, עָשָׂה הַמֶּלֶךְ
לְכָל-הָעָם הַנִּמְצְאִים
בְּשׁוּשַׁן הַבִּירָה לְמִגָּדוֹל
וְעַד-קָטָן מִשְׁתֶּה--שִׁבְעַת
יָמִים: בַּחֲצַר, גִּנַּת בִּיתַן
הַמֶּלֶךְ.

5 And when these days were fulfilled, the king made a feast unto all the people that were present in Shushan the castle, both great and small, seven days, in the court of the garden of the king's palace;

ו חוּר כַּרְפַּס וּתְכֵלֶת,
אָחוּז בְּחַבְלֵי-בוּץ
וְאַרְגָּמָן, עַל-גְּלִילֵי כֶסֶף,
וְעַמּוּדֵי שֵׁשׁ; מִטּוֹת זָהָב
וָכֶסֶף, עַל רִצְפַת בַּהַט-
וָשֵׁשׁ--וְדַר וְסֹחָרֶת.

6 there were hangings of white, fine cotton, and blue, bordered with cords of fine linen and purple, upon silver rods and pillars of marble; the couches were of gold and silver, upon a pavement of green, and white, and shell, and onyx marble.

ז וְהַשְׁקוֹת בִּכְלֵי זָהָב,
וְכֵלִים מִכֵּלִים שׁוֹנִים;
וְיֵין מַלְכוּת רָב, כְּיַד
הַמֶּלֶךְ.

7 And they gave them drink in vessels of gold--the vessels being diverse one from another--and royal wine in abundance, according to the bounty of the king.

ח וְהַשְּׁתִיָּה כַדָּת, אֵין אֹנֵס : כִּי-כֵן יִסַּד הַמֶּלֶךְ, עַל כָּל-רַב בֵּיתוֹ-- לַעֲשׂוֹת, כִּרְצוֹן אִישׁ-וָאִישׁ. {ס}

8 And the drinking wa according to the law; none di compel; for so the king had appointed to all the officers o his house, that they should d according to every man' pleasure. {S}

ט גַּם וַשְׁתִּי הַמַּלְכָּה, עָשְׂתָה מִשְׁתֵּה נָשִׁים-- בֵּית, הַמַּלְכוּת, אֲשֶׁר, לַמֶּלֶךְ אֲחַשְׁוֵרוֹשׁ.

9 Also Vashti the queen made a feast for the women in the royal house which belonged to king Ahasuerus.

י בַּיּוֹם, הַשְּׁבִיעִי, כְּטוֹב לֵב-הַמֶּלֶךְ, בַּיָּיִן--אָמַר לִמְהוּמָן בִּזְּתָא חַרְבוֹנָא בִּגְתָא וַאֲבַגְתָא, זֵתַר וְכַרְכַּס, שִׁבְעַת הַסָּרִיסִים, הַמְשָׁרְתִים אֶת-פְּנֵי הַמֶּלֶךְ אֲחַשְׁוֵרוֹשׁ.

10 On the seventh day, wher the heart of the king was merr with wine, he commanded Mehuman, Bizzetha Harbona, Bigtha, and Abagtha, Zethar, and Carcas the seven chamberlains that ministered in the presence o Ahasuerus the king,

יא לְהָבִיא אֶת-וַשְׁתִּי הַמַּלְכָּה, לִפְנֵי הַמֶּלֶךְ-- בְּכֶתֶר מַלְכוּת: לְהַרְאוֹת הָעַמִּים וְהַשָּׂרִים אֶת-יָפְיָהּ, כִּי-טוֹבַת מַרְאֶה הִיא.

11 to bring Vashti the queen before the king with the crown royal, to show the peoples and the princes her beauty; for she was fair to look on.

יב וַתְּמָאֵן הַמַּלְכָּה וַשְׁתִּי, לָבוֹא בִּדְבַר הַמֶּלֶךְ, אֲשֶׁר, בְּיַד הַסָּרִיסִים; וַיִּקְצֹף הַמֶּלֶךְ מְאֹד, וַחֲמָתוֹ בָּעֲרָה בוֹ. {ס}

12 But the queen Vashti refused to come at the king's commandment by the chamberlains; therefore was the king very wroth, and his anger burned in him. {S}

יג וַיֹּאמֶר הַמֶּלֶךְ, לַחֲכָמִים יֹדְעֵי הָעִתִּים: כִּי-כֵן, דְּבַר הַמֶּלֶךְ, לִפְנֵי, כָּל-יֹדְעֵי דָּת וָדִין.

13 Then the king said to the wise men, who knew the times--for so was the king's manner toward all that knew law and judgment;

יד וְהַקָּרֹב אֵלָיו, כַּרְשְׁנָא שֵׁתָר אַדְמָתָא תַרְשִׁישׁ, מֶרֶס מַרְסְנָא, מְמוּכָן-- שִׁבְעַת שָׂרֵי פָּרַס וּמָדַי, רֹאֵי פְּנֵי הַמֶּלֶךְ, הַיֹּשְׁבִים רִאשֹׁנָה, בַּמַּלְכוּת.

14 and the next unto him was Carshena, Shethar, Admatha, Tarshish, Meres, Marsena, and Memucan, the seven princes of Persia and Media, who saw the king's face, and sat the first in the kingdom:

טו כְּדָת, מַה-לַּעֲשׂוֹת, בַּמַּלְכָּה, וַשְׁתִּי--עַל אֲשֶׁר לֹא-עָשְׂתָה, אֶת-מַאֲמַר הַמֶּלֶךְ אֲחַשְׁוֵרוֹשׁ, בְּיַד, הַסָּרִיסִים. {ס}

15 'What shall we do unto the queen Vashti according to law, forasmuch as she hath not done the bidding of the king Ahasuerus by the chamberlains?' {S}

טז וַיֹּאמֶר מומכן (מְמוּכָן), לִפְנֵי הַמֶּלֶךְ וְהַשָּׂרִים, לֹא עַל-הַמֶּלֶךְ לְבַדּוֹ, עָוְתָה וַשְׁתִּי הַמַּלְכָּה: כִּי עַל-כָּל-הַשָּׂרִים, וְעַל-כָּל-הָעַמִּים, אֲשֶׁר, בְּכָל-מְדִינוֹת הַמֶּלֶךְ אֲחַשְׁוֵרוֹשׁ.

16 And Memucan answered before the king and the princes: 'Vashti the queen hath not done wrong to the king only, but also to all the princes, and to all the peoples, that are in all the provinces of the king Ahasuerus.

17 For this deed of the queen will come abroad unto all women, to make their husbands contemptible in their eyes, when it will be said: The king Ahasuerus commanded Vashti the queen to be brought in before him, but she came not.

יז כִּי-יֵצֵא דְבַר-הַמַּלְכָּה עַל-כָּל-הַנָּשִׁים, לְהַבְזוֹת בַּעְלֵיהֶן בְּעֵינֵיהֶן : בְּאָמְרָם, הַמֶּלֶךְ אֲחַשְׁוֵרוֹשׁ אָמַר לְהָבִיא אֶת-וַשְׁתִּי הַמַּלְכָּה לְפָנָיו-- וְלֹא-בָאָה.

18 And this day will the princesses of Persia and Media who have heard of the deed of the queen say the like unto all the king's princes. So will there arise enough contempt and wrath.

יח וְהַיּוֹם הַזֶּה תֹּאמַרְנָה שָׂרוֹת פָּרַס-וּמָדַי, אֲשֶׁר שָׁמְעוּ אֶת-דְּבַר הַמַּלְכָּה, לְכֹל, שָׂרֵי הַמֶּלֶךְ ; וּכְדַי, בִּזָּיוֹן וָקָצֶף.

19 If it please the king, let there go forth a royal commandment from him, and let it be written among the laws of the Persians and the Medes, that it be not altered, that Vashti come no more before king Ahasuerus, and that the king give her royal estate unto another that is better than she.

יט אִם-עַל-הַמֶּלֶךְ טוֹב, יֵצֵא דְבַר-מַלְכוּת מִלְּפָנָיו, וְיִכָּתֵב בְּדָתֵי פָרַס-וּמָדַי, וְלֹא יַעֲבוֹר : אֲשֶׁר לֹא-תָבוֹא וַשְׁתִּי, לִפְנֵי הַמֶּלֶךְ אֲחַשְׁוֵרוֹשׁ, וּמַלְכוּתָהּ יִתֵּן הַמֶּלֶךְ, לִרְעוּתָהּ הַטּוֹבָה מִמֶּנָּה.

20 And when the king's decree which he shall make shall be published throughout all his kingdom, great though it be, all the wives will give to their husbands honour, both to great and small.'

כ וְנִשְׁמַע פִּתְגָם הַמֶּלֶךְ אֲשֶׁר-יַעֲשֶׂה בְּכָל-מַלְכוּתוֹ, כִּי רַבָּה הִיא; וְכָל-הַנָּשִׁים, יִתְּנוּ יְקָר לְבַעְלֵיהֶן--לְמִגָּדוֹל, וְעַד-קָטָן.

21 And the word pleased the king and the princes; and the king did according to the word of Memucan;

כא וַיִּיטַב, הַדָּבָר, בְּעֵינֵי הַמֶּלֶךְ, וְהַשָּׂרִים; וַיַּעַשׂ הַמֶּלֶךְ, כִּדְבַר מְמוּכָן.

22 for he sent letters into all the king's provinces, into every province according to the writing thereof, and to every people after their language, that every man should bear rule in his own house, and speak according to the language of his people. {S}

כב וַיִּשְׁלַח סְפָרִים, אֶל-כָּל-מְדִינוֹת הַמֶּלֶךְ--אֶל-מְדִינָה וּמְדִינָה כִּכְתָבָהּ, וְאֶל-עַם וָעָם כִּלְשׁוֹנוֹ: לִהְיוֹת כָּל-אִישׁ שֹׂרֵר בְּבֵיתוֹ, וּמְדַבֵּר כִּלְשׁוֹן עַמּוֹ. {ס}

Esther Chapter 2 אֶסְתֵּר

א אַחַר, הַדְּבָרִים הָאֵלֶּה, כְּשֹׁךְ, חֲמַת הַמֶּלֶךְ אֲחַשְׁוֵרוֹשׁ--זָכַר אֶת-וַשְׁתִּי וְאֵת אֲשֶׁר-עָשָׂתָה, וְאֵת אֲשֶׁר-נִגְזַר עָלֶיהָ.

1 After these things, when the wrath of king Ahasuerus was assuaged, he remembered Vashti, and what she had done, and what was decreed against her.

ב וַיֹּאמְרוּ נַעֲרֵי-הַמֶּלֶךְ, מְשָׁרְתָיו : יְבַקְשׁוּ לַמֶּלֶךְ נְעָרוֹת בְּתוּלוֹת, טוֹבוֹת מַרְאֶה.

2 Then said the king's servants that ministered unto him: 'Let there be sought for the king young virgins fair to look on;

ג וְיַפְקֵד הַמֶּלֶךְ פְּקִידִים, בְּכָל-מְדִינוֹת מַלְכוּתוֹ, וְיִקְבְּצוּ אֶת-כָּל-נַעֲרָה-בְתוּלָה טוֹבַת מַרְאֶה אֶל-שׁוּשַׁן הַבִּירָה אֶל-בֵּית הַנָּשִׁים, אֶל-יַד הֵגֶא סְרִיס הַמֶּלֶךְ שֹׁמֵר הַנָּשִׁים ; וְנָתוֹן, תַּמְרֻקֵיהֶן.

3 and let the king appoint officers in all the provinces of his kingdom, that they may gather together all the fair young virgins unto Shushan the castle, to the house of the women, unto the custody of Hegai the king's chamberlain, keeper of the women; and let their ointments be given them;

4 and let the maiden that pleaseth the king be queen instead of Vashti.' And the thing pleased the king; and he did so. {S}

ד וְהַנַּעֲרָה, אֲשֶׁר תִּיטַב בְּעֵינֵי הַמֶּלֶךְ--תִּמְלֹךְ, תַּחַת וַשְׁתִּי ; וַיִּיטַב הַדָּבָר בְּעֵינֵי הַמֶּלֶךְ, וַיַּעַשׂ כֵּן. {ס}

5 There was a certain Jew in Shushan the castle, whose name was Mordecai the son of Jair the son of Shimei the son of Kish, a Benjamite,

ה אִישׁ יְהוּדִי, הָיָה בְּשׁוּשַׁן הַבִּירָה ; וּשְׁמוֹ מָרְדֳּכַי, בֶּן יָאִיר בֶּן-שִׁמְעִי בֶּן-קִישׁ--אִישׁ יְמִינִי.

6 who had been carried away from Jerusalem with the captives that had been carried away with Jeconiah king of Judah, whom Nebuchadnezzar the king of Babylon had carried away.

ו אֲשֶׁר הָגְלָה, מִירוּשָׁלַיִם, עִם-הַגֹּלָה אֲשֶׁר הָגְלְתָה, עִם יְכָנְיָה מֶלֶךְ-יְהוּדָה--אֲשֶׁר הֶגְלָה, נְבוּכַדְנֶצַּר מֶלֶךְ בָּבֶל.

7 And he brought up Hadassah, that is, Esther, his uncle's daughter; for she had neither father nor mother, and the maiden was of beautiful form and fair to look on; and when her father and mother were dead, Mordecai took her for his own daughter.

ז וַיְהִי אֹמֵן אֶת-הֲדַסָּה, הִיא אֶסְתֵּר בַּת-דֹּדוֹ--כִּי אֵין לָהּ, אָב וָאֵם ; וְהַנַּעֲרָה יְפַת-תֹּאַר, וְטוֹבַת מַרְאֶה, וּבְמוֹת אָבִיהָ וְאִמָּהּ, לְקָחָהּ מָרְדֳּכַי לוֹ לְבַת.

ח וַיְהִי, בְּהִשָּׁמַע דְּבַר-הַמֶּלֶךְ וְדָתוֹ, וּבְהִקָּבֵץ נְעָרוֹת רַבּוֹת אֶל-שׁוּשַׁן הַבִּירָה, אֶל-יַד הֵגָי; וַתִּלָּקַח אֶסְתֵּר אֶל-בֵּית הַמֶּלֶךְ, אֶל-יַד הֵגַי שֹׁמֵר הַנָּשִׁים.

8 So it came to pass, when the king's commandment and his decree was published, and when many maidens were gathered together unto Shushan the castle, to the custody of Hegai, that Esther was taken into the king's house, to the custody of Hegai, keeper of the women.

ט וַתִּיטַב הַנַּעֲרָה בְעֵינָיו, וַתִּשָּׂא חֶסֶד לְפָנָיו, וַיְבַהֵל אֶת-תַּמְרוּקֶיהָ וְאֶת-מָנוֹתֶהָ לָתֵת לָהּ, וְאֵת שֶׁבַע הַנְּעָרוֹת הָרְאֻיוֹת לָתֶת-לָהּ מִבֵּית הַמֶּלֶךְ; וַיְשַׁנֶּהָ וְאֶת-נַעֲרוֹתֶיהָ לְטוֹב, בֵּית הַנָּשִׁים.

9 And the maiden pleased him, and she obtained kindness of him; and he speedily gave her her ointments, with her portions, and the seven maidens, who were meet to be given her out of the king's house; and he advanced her and her maidens to the best place in the house of the women.

י לֹא-הִגִּידָה אֶסְתֵּר, אֶת-עַמָּהּ וְאֶת-מוֹלַדְתָּהּ: כִּי מָרְדֳּכַי צִוָּה עָלֶיהָ, אֲשֶׁר לֹא-תַגִּיד.

10 Esther had not made known her people nor her kindred; for Mordecai had charged her that she should not tell it.

יא וּבְכָל-יוֹם וָיוֹם--
מָרְדֳּכַי מִתְהַלֵּךְ, לִפְנֵי
חֲצַר בֵּית-
הַנָּשִׁים : לָדַעַת אֶת-
שְׁלוֹם אֶסְתֵּר, וּמַה-
יֵּעָשֶׂה בָּהּ.

11 And Mordecai walked every day before the court of the women's house, to know how Esther did, and what would become of her.

יב וּבְהַגִּיעַ תֹּר נַעֲרָה
וְנַעֲרָה לָבוֹא אֶל-הַמֶּלֶךְ
אֲחַשְׁוֵרוֹשׁ, מִקֵּץ הֱיוֹת
לָהּ כְּדָת הַנָּשִׁים שְׁנֵים
עָשָׂר חֹדֶשׁ--כִּי כֵּן
יִמְלְאוּ, יְמֵי
מְרוּקֵיהֶן : שִׁשָּׁה
חֳדָשִׁים, בְּשֶׁמֶן הַמֹּר,
וְשִׁשָּׁה חֳדָשִׁים
בַּבְּשָׂמִים, וּבְתַמְרוּקֵי
הַנָּשִׁים.

12 Now when the turn of every maiden was come to go in to king Ahasuerus, after that it had been done to her according to the law for the women, twelve months-- for so were the days of their anointing accomplished, to wit, six months with oil of myrrh, and six month with sweet odours, and with other ointments of the women--

יג וּבָזֶה, הַנַּעֲרָה בָּאָה
אֶל-הַמֶּלֶךְ--אֶת כָּל-
אֲשֶׁר תֹּאמַר יִנָּתֵן לָהּ,
לָבוֹא עִמָּהּ, מִבֵּית
הַנָּשִׁים, עַד-בֵּית הַמֶּלֶךְ.

13 when then the maiden came unto the king, whatsoever she desired was given her to go with her out of the house of the women unto the king's house.

14 In the evening she went, and on the morrow she returned into the second house of the women, to the custody of Shaashgaz, the king's chamberlain, who kept the concubines; she came in unto the king no more, except the king delighted in her, and she were called by name.

יד בָּעֶרֶב הִיא בָאָה, וּבַבֹּקֶר הִיא שָׁבָה אֶל-בֵּית הַנָּשִׁים שֵׁנִי, אֶל-יַד שַׁעַשְׁגַז סְרִיס הַמֶּלֶךְ, שֹׁמֵר הַפִּילַגְשִׁים: לֹא-תָבוֹא עוֹד אֶל-הַמֶּלֶךְ, כִּי אִם-חָפֵץ בָּהּ הַמֶּלֶךְ וְנִקְרְאָה בְשֵׁם.

15 Now when the turn of Esther, the daughter of Abihail the uncle of Mordecai, who had taken her for his daughter, was come to go in unto the king, she required nothing but what Hegai the king's chamberlain, the keeper of the women, appointed. And Esther obtained favour in the sight of all them that looked upon her.

טו וּבְהַגִּיעַ תֹּר-אֶסְתֵּר בַּת-אֲבִיחַיִל דֹּד מָרְדֳּכַי אֲשֶׁר לָקַח-לוֹ לְבַת לָבוֹא אֶל-הַמֶּלֶךְ, לֹא בִקְשָׁה דָּבָר--כִּי אִם אֶת-אֲשֶׁר יֹאמַר הֵגַי סְרִיס-הַמֶּלֶךְ, שֹׁמֵר הַנָּשִׁים; וַתְּהִי אֶסְתֵּר נֹשֵׂאת חֵן, בְּעֵינֵי כָּל-רֹאֶיהָ.

16 So Esther was taken unto king Ahasuerus into his house royal in the tenth month, which is the month Tebeth, in the seventh year of his reign.

טז וַתִּלָּקַח אֶסְתֵּר אֶל-הַמֶּלֶךְ אֲחַשְׁוֵרוֹשׁ, אֶל-בֵּית מַלְכוּתוֹ, בַּחֹדֶשׁ הָעֲשִׂירִי, הוּא-חֹדֶשׁ טֵבֵת--בִּשְׁנַת-שֶׁבַע, לְמַלְכוּתוֹ.

יז וַיֶּאֱהַב הַמֶּלֶךְ אֶת-אֶסְתֵּר מִכָּל-הַנָּשִׁים, וַתִּשָּׂא-חֵן וָחֶסֶד לְפָנָיו מִכָּל-הַבְּתוּלוֹת; וַיָּשֶׂם כֶּתֶר-מַלְכוּת בְּרֹאשָׁהּ, וַיַּמְלִיכֶהָ תַּחַת וַשְׁתִּי.

17 And the king loved Esthe above all the women, and she obtained grace and favour in hi sight more than all the virgins so that he set the royal crown upon her head, and made he queen instead of Vashti.

יח וַיַּעַשׂ הַמֶּלֶךְ מִשְׁתֶּה גָדוֹל, לְכָל-שָׂרָיו וַעֲבָדָיו-אֶת, מִשְׁתֵּה אֶסְתֵּר; וַהֲנָחָה לַמְּדִינוֹת עָשָׂה, וַיִּתֵּן מַשְׂאֵת כְּיַד הַמֶּלֶךְ.

18 Then the king made a great feast unto all his princes and his servants, even Esther's feast; and he made a release to the provinces, and gave gifts, according to the bounty of the king.

יט וּבְהִקָּבֵץ בְּתוּלוֹת, שֵׁנִית; וּמָרְדֳּכַי, יֹשֵׁב בְּשַׁעַר-הַמֶּלֶךְ.

19 And when the virgins were gathered together the second time, and Mordecai sat in the king's gate--

כ אֵין אֶסְתֵּר, מַגֶּדֶת מוֹלַדְתָּהּ וְאֶת-עַמָּהּ, כַּאֲשֶׁר צִוָּה עָלֶיהָ, מָרְדֳּכָי; וְאֶת-מַאֲמַר מָרְדֳּכַי אֶסְתֵּר עֹשָׂה, כַּאֲשֶׁר הָיְתָה בְאָמְנָה אִתּוֹ. {ס}

20 Esther had not yet made known her kindred nor her people; as Mordecai had charged her; for Esther did the commandment of Mordecai, like as when she was brought up with him-- {S}

כא בַּיָּמִים הָהֵם, וּמָרְדֳּכַי יוֹשֵׁב בְּשַׁעַר-הַמֶּלֶךְ; קָצַף בִּגְתָן וָתֶרֶשׁ שְׁנֵי-סָרִיסֵי הַמֶּלֶךְ, מִשֹּׁמְרֵי הַסַּף, וַיְבַקְשׁוּ לִשְׁלֹחַ יָד, בַּמֶּלֶךְ אֲחַשְׁוֵרֹשׁ.

21 in those days, while Mordecai sat in the king's gate, two of the king's chamberlains, Bigthan and Teresh, of those that kept the door, were wroth, and sought to lay hands on the king Ahasuerus.

כב וַיִּוָּדַע הַדָּבָר לְמָרְדֳּכַי, וַיַּגֵּד לְאֶסְתֵּר הַמַּלְכָּה; וַתֹּאמֶר אֶסְתֵּר לַמֶּלֶךְ, בְּשֵׁם מָרְדֳּכָי.

22 And the thing became known to Mordecai, who told it unto Esther the queen; and Esther told the king thereof in Mordecai's name.

כג וַיְבֻקַּשׁ הַדָּבָר וַיִּמָּצֵא, וַיִּתָּלוּ שְׁנֵיהֶם עַל-עֵץ; וַיִּכָּתֵב, בְּסֵפֶר דִּבְרֵי הַיָּמִים--לִפְנֵי הַמֶּלֶךְ. {ס}

23 And when inquisition was made of the matter, and it was found to be so, they were both hanged on a tree; and it was written in the book of the chronicles before the king. {S}

Esther Chapter 3 אֶסְתֵּר

א אַחַר הַדְּבָרִים הָאֵלֶּה, גִּדַּל הַמֶּלֶךְ אֲחַשְׁוֵרוֹשׁ אֶת-הָמָן בֶּן-הַמְּדָתָא הָאֲגָגִי-וַיְנַשְּׂאֵהוּ ; וַיָּשֶׂם, אֶת-כִּסְאוֹ, מֵעַל, כָּל-הַשָּׂרִים אֲשֶׁר אִתּוֹ.

1 After these things did king Ahasuerus promote Haman the son of Hammedatha the Agagite, and advanced him, and set his seat above all the princes that were with him.

ב וְכָל-עַבְדֵי הַמֶּלֶךְ אֲשֶׁר-בְּשַׁעַר הַמֶּלֶךְ, כֹּרְעִים וּמִשְׁתַּחֲוִים לְהָמָן--כִּי-כֵן, צִוָּה-לוֹ הַמֶּלֶךְ ; וּמָרְדֳּכַי--לֹא יִכְרַע, וְלֹא יִשְׁתַּחֲוֶה.

2 And all the king's servants, that were in the king's gate, bowed down, and prostrated themselves before Haman; for the king had so commanded concerning him. But Mordecai bowed not down, nor prostrated himself before him.

ג וַיֹּאמְרוּ עַבְדֵי הַמֶּלֶךְ, אֲשֶׁר-בְּשַׁעַר הַמֶּלֶךְ-- לְמָרְדֳּכָי : מַדּוּעַ אַתָּה עוֹבֵר, אֵת מִצְוַת הַמֶּלֶךְ.

3 Then the king's servants, that were in the king's gate, said unto Mordecai: 'Why transgressest thou the king's commandment?'

ד וַיְהִי, בְּאָמְרָם (כְּאָמְרָם) אֵלָיו יוֹם וָיוֹם, וְלֹא שָׁמַע, אֲלֵיהֶם; וַיַּגִּידוּ לְהָמָן, לִרְאוֹת הֲיַעַמְדוּ דִּבְרֵי מָרְדֳּכַי--כִּי-הִגִּיד לָהֶם, אֲשֶׁר-הוּא יְהוּדִי.

4 Now it came to pass, when they spoke daily unto him, and he hearkened not unto them, that they told Haman, to see whether Mordecai's words would stand; for he had told them that he was a Jew.

ה וַיַּרְא הָמָן--כִּי-אֵין מָרְדֳּכַי, כֹּרֵעַ וּמִשְׁתַּחֲוֶה לוֹ; וַיִּמָּלֵא הָמָן, חֵמָה.

5 And when Haman saw that Mordecai bowed not down, nor prostrated himself before him, then was Haman full of wrath.

ו וַיִּבֶז בְּעֵינָיו, לִשְׁלֹחַ יָד בְּמָרְדֳּכַי לְבַדּוֹ--כִּי-הִגִּידוּ לוֹ, אֶת-עַם מָרְדֳּכָי; וַיְבַקֵּשׁ הָמָן, לְהַשְׁמִיד אֶת-כָּל-הַיְּהוּדִים אֲשֶׁר בְּכָל-מַלְכוּת אֲחַשְׁוֵרוֹשׁ--עַם מָרְדֳּכָי.

6 But it seemed contemptible in his eyes to lay hands on Mordecai alone; for they had made known to him the people of Mordecai; wherefore Haman sought to destroy all the Jews that were throughout the whole kingdom of Ahasuerus, even the people of Mordecai.

7 In the first month, which is the month Nisan, in the twelfth year of king Ahasuerus, they cast pur, that is, the lot, before Haman from day to day, and from month to month, to the twelfth month, which is the month Adar. {S}

ז בַּחֹדֶשׁ הָרִאשׁוֹן, הוּא-חֹדֶשׁ נִיסָן, בִּשְׁנַת שְׁתֵּים עֶשְׂרֵה, לַמֶּלֶךְ אֲחַשְׁוֵרוֹשׁ: הִפִּיל פּוּר הוּא הַגּוֹרָל לִפְנֵי הָמָן, מִיּוֹם לְיוֹם וּמֵחֹדֶשׁ לְחֹדֶשׁ שְׁנֵים-עָשָׂר--הוּא-חֹדֶשׁ אֲדָר. {ס}

8 And Haman said unto king Ahasuerus: 'There is a certain people scattered abroad and dispersed among the peoples in all the provinces of thy kingdom; and their laws are diverse from those of every people; neither keep they the king's laws; therefore it profiteth not the king to suffer them.

ח וַיֹּאמֶר הָמָן, לַמֶּלֶךְ אֲחַשְׁוֵרוֹשׁ--יֶשְׁנוֹ עַם-אֶחָד מְפֻזָּר וּמְפֹרָד בֵּין הָעַמִּים, בְּכֹל מְדִינוֹת מַלְכוּתֶךָ; וְדָתֵיהֶם שֹׁנוֹת מִכָּל-עָם, וְאֶת-דָּתֵי הַמֶּלֶךְ אֵינָם עֹשִׂים, וְלַמֶּלֶךְ אֵין-שֹׁוֶה, לְהַנִּיחָם.

9 If it please the king, let it be written that they be destroyed; and I will pay ten thousand talents of silver into the hands of those that have the charge of the king's business, to bring it into the king's treasuries.'

ט אִם-עַל-הַמֶּלֶךְ טוֹב, יִכָּתֵב לְאַבְּדָם; וַעֲשֶׂרֶת אֲלָפִים כִּכַּר-כֶּסֶף, אֶשְׁקוֹל עַל-יְדֵי עֹשֵׂי הַמְּלָאכָה, לְהָבִיא, אֶל-גִּנְזֵי הַמֶּלֶךְ.

10 And the king took his ring from his hand, and gave it unto Haman the son of Hammedatha the Agagite, the Jews' enemy.

11 And the king said unto Haman: 'The silver is given to thee, the people also, to do with them as it seemeth good to thee.'

12 Then were the king's scribes called in the first month, on the thirteenth day thereof, and there was written, according to all that Haman commanded, unto the king's satraps, and to the governors that were over every province, and to the princes of every people; to every province according to the writing thereof, and to every people after their language; in the name of king Ahasuerus was it written, and it was sealed with the king's ring.

י וַיָּסַר הַמֶּלֶךְ אֶת-טַבַּעְתּוֹ, מֵעַל יָדוֹ; וַיִּתְּנָהּ, לְהָמָן בֶּן-הַמְּדָתָא הָאֲגָגִי--צֹרֵר הַיְּהוּדִים.

יא וַיֹּאמֶר הַמֶּלֶךְ לְהָמָן, הַכֶּסֶף נָתוּן לָךְ; וְהָעָם, לַעֲשׂוֹת בּוֹ כַּטּוֹב בְּעֵינֶיךָ.

יב וַיִּקָּרְאוּ סֹפְרֵי הַמֶּלֶךְ בַּחֹדֶשׁ הָרִאשׁוֹן, בִּשְׁלוֹשָׁה עָשָׂר יוֹם בּוֹ, וַיִּכָּתֵב כְּכָל-אֲשֶׁר-צִוָּה הָמָן אֶל אֲחַשְׁדַּרְפְּנֵי-הַמֶּלֶךְ וְאֶל-הַפַּחוֹת אֲשֶׁר עַל-מְדִינָה וּמְדִינָה וְאֶל-שָׂרֵי עַם וָעָם, מְדִינָה וּמְדִינָה כִּכְתָבָהּ וְעַם וָעָם כִּלְשׁוֹנוֹ: בְּשֵׁם הַמֶּלֶךְ אֲחַשְׁוֵרֹשׁ נִכְתָּב, וְנֶחְתָּם בְּטַבַּעַת הַמֶּלֶךְ.

יג וְנִשְׁלוֹחַ סְפָרִים בְּיַד הָרָצִים, אֶל-כָּל-מְדִינוֹת הַמֶּלֶךְ--לְהַשְׁמִיד לַהֲרֹג וּלְאַבֵּד אֶת-כָּל-הַיְּהוּדִים מִנַּעַר וְעַד-זָקֵן טַף וְנָשִׁים בְּיוֹם אֶחָד, בִּשְׁלוֹשָׁה עָשָׂר לְחֹדֶשׁ שְׁנֵים-עָשָׂר הוּא-חֹדֶשׁ אֲדָר; וּשְׁלָלָם, לָבוֹז.

יד פַּתְשֶׁגֶן הַכְּתָב, לְהִנָּתֵן דָּת בְּכָל-מְדִינָה וּמְדִינָה, גָּלוּי, לְכָל-הָעַמִּים--לִהְיוֹת עֲתִדִים, לַיּוֹם הַזֶּה.

טו הָרָצִים יָצְאוּ דְחוּפִים, בִּדְבַר הַמֶּלֶךְ, וְהַדָּת נִתְּנָה, בְּשׁוּשַׁן הַבִּירָה; וְהַמֶּלֶךְ וְהָמָן יָשְׁבוּ לִשְׁתּוֹת, וְהָעִיר שׁוּשָׁן נָבוֹכָה. {ס}

13 And letters were sent by posts into all the king's provinces, to destroy, to slay, and to cause to perish, all Jews, both young and old, little children and women, in one day, even upon the thirteenth day of the twelfth month, which is the month Adar, and to take the spoil of them for a prey.

14 The copy of the writing, to be given out for a decree in every province, was to be published unto all peoples, that they should be ready against that day.

15 The posts went forth in haste by the king's commandment, and the decree was given out in Shushan the castle; and the king and Haman sat down to drink; but the city of Shushan was perplexed. {S}

Esther Chapter 4 אֶסְתֵּר

א וּמָרְדֳּכַי, יָדַע אֶת-כָּל-אֲשֶׁר נַעֲשָׂה, וַיִּקְרַע מָרְדֳּכַי אֶת-בְּגָדָיו, וַיִּלְבַּשׁ שַׂק וָאֵפֶר; וַיֵּצֵא בְּתוֹךְ הָעִיר, וַיִּזְעַק זְעָקָה גְדוֹלָה וּמָרָה.

1 Now when Mordecai knew all that was done, Mordecai rent his clothes, and put on sackcloth with ashes, and went out into the midst of the city, and cried with a loud and a bitter cry;

ב וַיָּבוֹא, עַד לִפְנֵי שַׁעַר-הַמֶּלֶךְ : כִּי אֵין לָבוֹא אֶל-שַׁעַר הַמֶּלֶךְ, בִּלְבוּשׁ שָׂק.

2 and he came even before the king's gate; for none might enter within the king's gate clothed with sackcloth.

ג וּבְכָל-מְדִינָה וּמְדִינָה, מְקוֹם אֲשֶׁר דְּבַר-הַמֶּלֶךְ וְדָתוֹ מַגִּיעַ--אֵבֶל גָּדוֹל לַיְּהוּדִים, וְצוֹם וּבְכִי וּמִסְפֵּד; שַׂק וָאֵפֶר, יֻצַּע לָרַבִּים.

3 And in every province, whithersoever the king's commandment and his decree came, there was great mourning among the Jews, and fasting, and weeping, and wailing; and many lay in sackcloth and ashes.

ד ותבואינה (וַתָּבוֹאנָה) נַעֲרוֹת אֶסְתֵּר וְסָרִיסֶיהָ, וַיַּגִּידוּ לָהּ, וַתִּתְחַלְחַל הַמַּלְכָּה, מְאֹד; וַתִּשְׁלַח בְּגָדִים לְהַלְבִּישׁ אֶת-מָרְדֳּכַי, וּלְהָסִיר שַׂקּוֹ מֵעָלָיו--וְלֹא קִבֵּל.

4 And Esther's maidens and her chamberlains came and told it her; and the queen was exceedingly pained; and she sent raiment to clothe Mordecai; and to take his sackcloth from off him; but he accepted it not.

5 Then called Esther for Hathach, one of the king's chamberlains, whom he had appointed to attend upon her, and charged him to go to Mordecai, to know what this was, and why it was.

ה וַתִּקְרָא אֶסְתֵּר לַהֲתָךְ מִסָּרִיסֵי הַמֶּלֶךְ, אֲשֶׁר הֶעֱמִיד לְפָנֶיהָ, וַתְּצַוֵּהוּ, עַל-מָרְדֳּכָי--לָדַעַת מַה-זֶּה, וְעַל-מַה-זֶּה.

6 So Hathach went forth to Mordecai unto the broad place of the city, which was before the king's gate.

ו וַיֵּצֵא הֲתָךְ, אֶל-מָרְדֳּכָי--אֶל-רְחוֹב הָעִיר, אֲשֶׁר לִפְנֵי שַׁעַר-הַמֶּלֶךְ.

7 And Mordecai told him of all that had happened unto him, and the exact sum of the money that Haman had promised to pay to the king's treasuries for the Jews, to destroy them.

ז וַיַּגֶּד-לוֹ מָרְדֳּכַי, אֵת כָּל-אֲשֶׁר קָרָהוּ; וְאֵת פָּרָשַׁת הַכֶּסֶף, אֲשֶׁר אָמַר הָמָן לִשְׁקוֹל עַל-גִּנְזֵי הַמֶּלֶךְ ביהודיים (בַּיְּהוּדִים)--לְאַבְּדָם.

8 Also he gave him the copy of the writing of the decree that was given out in Shushan to destroy them, to show it unto Esther, and to declare it unto her; and to charge her that she should go in unto the king, to make supplication unto him, and to make request before him, for her people.

ח וְאֶת-פַּתְשֶׁגֶן כְּתָב-הַדָּת אֲשֶׁר-נִתַּן בְּשׁוּשָׁן לְהַשְׁמִידָם, נָתַן לוֹ--לְהַרְאוֹת אֶת-אֶסְתֵּר, וּלְהַגִּיד לָהּ; וּלְצַוּוֹת עָלֶיהָ, לָבוֹא אֶל-הַמֶּלֶךְ לְהִתְחַנֶּן-לוֹ וּלְבַקֵּשׁ מִלְּפָנָיו--עַל-עַמָּהּ.

ט וַיָּבוֹא, הֲתָךְ ; וַיַּגֵּד לְאֶסְתֵּר, אֵת דִּבְרֵי מָרְדֳּכָי.

9 And Hathach came and told Esther the words of Mordecai.

י וַתֹּאמֶר אֶסְתֵּר לַהֲתָךְ, וַתְּצַוֵּהוּ אֶל-מָרְדֳּכָי.

10 Then Esther spoke unto Hathach, and gave him a message unto Mordecai:

יא כָּל-עַבְדֵי הַמֶּלֶךְ וְעַם-מְדִינוֹת הַמֶּלֶךְ יֹדְעִים, אֲשֶׁר כָּל-אִישׁ וְאִשָּׁה אֲשֶׁר יָבוֹא-אֶל-הַמֶּלֶךְ אֶל-הֶחָצֵר הַפְּנִימִית אֲשֶׁר לֹא-יִקָּרֵא אַחַת דָּתוֹ לְהָמִית, לְבַד מֵאֲשֶׁר יוֹשִׁיט-לוֹ הַמֶּלֶךְ אֶת-שַׁרְבִיט הַזָּהָב, וְחָיָה ; וַאֲנִי, לֹא נִקְרֵאתִי לָבוֹא אֶל-הַמֶּלֶךְ--זֶה, שְׁלוֹשִׁים יוֹם.

11 'All the king's servants, and the people of the king's provinces, do know, that whosoever, whether man or woman, shall come unto the king into the inner court, who is not called, there is one law for him, that he be put to death, except such to whom the king shall hold out the golden sceptre, that he may live; but I have not been called to come in unto the king these thirty days.'

יב וַיַּגִּידוּ לְמָרְדֳּכָי, אֵת דִּבְרֵי אֶסְתֵּר.

12 And they told to Mordecai Esther's words.

יג וַיֹּאמֶר מָרְדֳּכַי, לְהָשִׁיב אֶל-אֶסְתֵּר : אַל-תְּדַמִּי בְנַפְשֵׁךְ, לְהִמָּלֵט בֵּית-הַמֶּלֶךְ מִכָּל-הַיְּהוּדִים.

13 Then Mordecai bade them to return answer unto Esther: 'Think not with thyself that thou shalt escape in the king's house, more than all the Jews.

יד כִּי אִם-הַחֲרֵשׁ
תַּחֲרִישִׁי, בָּעֵת הַזֹּאת--
רֶוַח וְהַצָּלָה יַעֲמוֹד
לַיְּהוּדִים מִמָּקוֹם אַחֵר,
וְאַתְּ וּבֵית-אָבִיךְ תֹּאבֵדוּ;
וּמִי יוֹדֵעַ--אִם-לְעֵת
כָּזֹאת, הִגַּעַתְּ לַמַּלְכוּת.

14 For if thou altogether holdest thy peace at this time, then will relief and deliverance arise to the Jews from another place, but thou and thy father's house will perish; and who knoweth whether thou art not come to royal estate for such a time as this?'

טו וַתֹּאמֶר אֶסְתֵּר,
לְהָשִׁיב אֶל-מָרְדֳּכָי.

15 Then Esther bade them return answer unto Mordecai:

טז לֵךְ כְּנוֹס אֶת-כָּל-
הַיְּהוּדִים הַנִּמְצְאִים
בְּשׁוּשָׁן, וְצוּמוּ עָלַי וְאַל-
תֹּאכְלוּ וְאַל-תִּשְׁתּוּ
שְׁלֹשֶׁת יָמִים לַיְלָה וָיוֹם-
-גַּם-אֲנִי וְנַעֲרֹתַי, אָצוּם
כֵּן; וּבְכֵן אָבוֹא אֶל-
הַמֶּלֶךְ, אֲשֶׁר לֹא-כַדָּת,
וְכַאֲשֶׁר אָבַדְתִּי, אָבָדְתִּי.

16 'Go, gather together all the Jews that are present in Shushan, and fast ye for me, and neither eat nor drink three days, night or day; I also and my maidens will fast in like manner; and so will I go in unto the king, which is not according to the law; and if I perish, I perish.'

יז וַיַּעֲבֹר, מָרְדֳּכָי; וַיַּעַשׂ,
כְּכֹל אֲשֶׁר-צִוְּתָה עָלָיו
אֶסְתֵּר.

17 So Mordecai went his way, and did according to all that Esther had commanded him.

Esther Chapter 5 אֶסְתֵּר

א וַיְהִי בַּיּוֹם הַשְּׁלִישִׁי, וַתִּלְבַּשׁ אֶסְתֵּר מַלְכוּת, וַתַּעֲמֹד בַּחֲצַר בֵּית-הַמֶּלֶךְ הַפְּנִימִית, נֹכַח בֵּית הַמֶּלֶךְ; וְהַמֶּלֶךְ יוֹשֵׁב עַל-כִּסֵּא מַלְכוּתוֹ, בְּבֵית הַמַּלְכוּת, נֹכַח, פֶּתַח הַבָּיִת.

1 Now it came to pass on the third day, that Esther put on her royal apparel, and stood in the inner court of the king's house, over against the king's house; and the king sat upon his royal throne in the royal house, over against the entrance of the house.

ב וַיְהִי כִרְאוֹת הַמֶּלֶךְ אֶת-אֶסְתֵּר הַמַּלְכָּה, עֹמֶדֶת בֶּחָצֵר--נָשְׂאָה חֵן, בְּעֵינָיו; וַיּוֹשֶׁט הַמֶּלֶךְ לְאֶסְתֵּר, אֶת-שַׁרְבִיט הַזָּהָב אֲשֶׁר בְּיָדוֹ, וַתִּקְרַב אֶסְתֵּר, וַתִּגַּע בְּרֹאשׁ הַשַּׁרְבִיט.

2 And it was so, when the king saw Esther the queen standing in the court, that she obtained favour in his sight; and the king held out to Esther the golden sceptre that was in his hand. So Esther drew near, and touched the top of the sceptre.

ג וַיֹּאמֶר לָהּ הַמֶּלֶךְ, מַה-לָּךְ אֶסְתֵּר הַמַּלְכָּה; וּמַה-בַּקָּשָׁתֵךְ עַד-חֲצִי הַמַּלְכוּת, וְיִנָּתֵן לָךְ.

3 Then said the king unto her: 'What wilt thou, queen Esther? for whatever thy request, even to the half of the kingdom, it shall be given thee.'

ד וַתֹּאמֶר אֶסְתֵּר, אִם-עַל-הַמֶּלֶךְ טוֹב--יָבוֹא הַמֶּלֶךְ וְהָמָן הַיּוֹם, אֶל-הַמִּשְׁתֶּה אֲשֶׁר-עָשִׂיתִי לוֹ.

4 And Esther said: 'If it seem good unto the king, let the king and Haman come this day unto the banquet that I have prepared for him.'

ה וַיֹּאמֶר הַמֶּלֶךְ--מַהֲרוּ אֶת-הָמָן, לַעֲשׂוֹת אֶת-דְּבַר אֶסְתֵּר ; וַיָּבֹא הַמֶּלֶךְ וְהָמָן, אֶל-הַמִּשְׁתֶּה אֲשֶׁר-עָשְׂתָה אֶסְתֵּר.

5 Then the king said: 'Cause Haman to make haste, that it may be done as Esther hath said.' So the king and Haman came to the banquet that Esther had prepared.

ו וַיֹּאמֶר הַמֶּלֶךְ לְאֶסְתֵּר בְּמִשְׁתֶּה הַיַּיִן, מַה-שְּׁאֵלָתֵךְ וְיִנָּתֵן לָךְ ; וּמַה-בַּקָּשָׁתֵךְ עַד-חֲצִי הַמַּלְכוּת, וְתֵעָשׂ.

6 And the king said unto Esther at the banquet of wine: 'Whatever thy petition, it shall be granted thee; and whatever thy request, even to the half of the kingdom, it shall be performed.'

ז וַתַּעַן אֶסְתֵּר, וַתֹּאמַר : שְׁאֵלָתִי, וּבַקָּשָׁתִי.

7 Then answered Esther, and said: 'My petition and my request is—

8 if I have found favour in the sight of the king, and if it please the king to grant my petition, and to perform my request--let the king and Haman come to the banquet that I shall prepare for them, and I will do to-morrow as the king hath said.'

ח אִם-מָצָאתִי חֵן בְּעֵינֵי הַמֶּלֶךְ, וְאִם-עַל-הַמֶּלֶךְ טוֹב, לָתֵת אֶת-שְׁאֵלָתִי, וְלַעֲשׂוֹת אֶת-בַּקָּשָׁתִי-- יָבוֹא הַמֶּלֶךְ וְהָמָן, אֶל-הַמִּשְׁתֶּה אֲשֶׁר אֶעֱשֶׂה לָהֶם, וּמָחָר אֶעֱשֶׂה, כִּדְבַר הַמֶּלֶךְ.

9 Then went Haman forth that day joyful and glad of heart; but when Haman saw Mordecai in the king's gate, that he stood not up, nor moved for him, Haman was filled with wrath against Mordecai.

ט וַיֵּצֵא הָמָן בַּיּוֹם הַהוּא, שָׂמֵחַ וְטוֹב לֵב; וְכִרְאוֹת הָמָן אֶת-מָרְדֳּכַי בְּשַׁעַר הַמֶּלֶךְ, וְלֹא-קָם וְלֹא-זָע מִמֶּנּוּ-- וַיִּמָּלֵא הָמָן עַל-מָרְדֳּכַי, חֵמָה.

10 Nevertheless Haman refrained himself, and went home; and he sent and fetched his friends and Zeresh his wife.

י וַיִּתְאַפַּק הָמָן, וַיָּבוֹא אֶל-בֵּיתוֹ; וַיִּשְׁלַח וַיָּבֵא אֶת-אֹהֲבָיו, וְאֶת-זֶרֶשׁ אִשְׁתּוֹ.

11 And Haman recounted unto them the glory of his riches, and the multitude of his children, and everything as to how the king had promoted him, and how he had advanced him above the princes and servants of the king.

יא וַיְסַפֵּר לָהֶם הָמָן אֶת-כְּבוֹד עָשְׁרוֹ, וְרֹב בָּנָיו ; וְאֵת כָּל-אֲשֶׁר גִּדְּלוֹ הַמֶּלֶךְ וְאֵת אֲשֶׁר נִשְּׂאוֹ, עַל-הַשָּׂרִים וְעַבְדֵי הַמֶּלֶךְ.

12 Haman said moreover: 'Yea, Esther the queen did let no man come in with the king unto the banquet that she had prepared but myself; and to-morrow also am I invited by her together with the king.

יב וַיֹּאמֶר, הָמָן--אַף לֹא-הֵבִיאָה אֶסְתֵּר הַמַּלְכָּה עִם-הַמֶּלֶךְ אֶל-הַמִּשְׁתֶּה אֲשֶׁר-עָשָׂתָה, כִּי אִם-אוֹתִי ; וְגַם-לְמָחָר אֲנִי קָרוּא-לָהּ, עִם-הַמֶּלֶךְ.

13 Yet all this availeth me nothing, so long as I see Mordecai the Jew sitting at the king's gate.'

יג וְכָל-זֶה, אֵינֶנּוּ שֹׁוֶה לִי : בְּכָל-עֵת, אֲשֶׁר אֲנִי רֹאֶה אֶת-מָרְדֳּכַי הַיְּהוּדִי--יוֹשֵׁב, בְּשַׁעַר הַמֶּלֶךְ.

יד וַתֹּאמֶר לוֹ זֶרֶשׁ אִשְׁתּוֹ וְכָל-אֹהֲבָיו, יַעֲשׂוּ-עֵץ גָּבֹהַּ חֲמִשִּׁים אַמָּה, וּבַבֹּקֶר אֱמֹר לַמֶּלֶךְ וְיִתְלוּ אֶת-מָרְדֳּכַי עָלָיו, וּבֹא-עִם-הַמֶּלֶךְ אֶל-הַמִּשְׁתֶּה שָׂמֵחַ; וַיִּיטַב הַדָּבָר לִפְנֵי הָמָן, וַיַּעַשׂ הָעֵץ. {ס}

14 Then said Zeresh his wife and all his friends unto him: 'Let a gallows be made of fifty cubits high, and in the morning speak thou unto the king that Mordecai may be hanged thereon; then go thou in merrily with the king unto the banquet.' And the thing pleased Haman; and he caused the gallows to be made. {S}

Esther Chapter 6 אֶסְתֵּר

א בַּלַּיְלָה הַהוּא, נָדְדָה שְׁנַת הַמֶּלֶךְ; וַיֹּאמֶר, לְהָבִיא אֶת-סֵפֶר הַזִּכְרֹנוֹת דִּבְרֵי הַיָּמִים, וַיִּהְיוּ נִקְרָאִים, לִפְנֵי הַמֶּלֶךְ.

1 On that night could not the king sleep; and he commanded to bring the book of records of the chronicles, and they were read before the king.

ב וַיִּמָּצֵא כָתוּב, אֲשֶׁר הִגִּיד מָרְדֳּכַי עַל-בִּגְתָנָא וָתֶרֶשׁ שְׁנֵי סָרִיסֵי הַמֶּלֶךְ--מִשֹּׁמְרֵי, הַסַּף: אֲשֶׁר בִּקְשׁוּ לִשְׁלֹחַ יָד, בַּמֶּלֶךְ אֲחַשְׁוֵרוֹשׁ.

2 And it was found written, that Mordecai had told of Bigthana and Teresh, two of the king's chamberlains, of those that kept the door, who had sought to lay hands on the king Ahasuerus.

ג וַיֹּאמֶר הַמֶּלֶךְ--מַה-נַּעֲשָׂה יְקָר וּגְדוּלָּה לְמָרְדֳּכַי, עַל-זֶה; וַיֹּאמְרוּ נַעֲרֵי הַמֶּלֶךְ, מְשָׁרְתָיו, לֹא-נַעֲשָׂה עִמּוֹ, דָּבָר.

3 And the king said: 'What honour and dignity hath been done to Mordecai for this?' Then said the king's servants that ministered unto him: 'There is nothing done for him.'

ד וַיֹּאמֶר הַמֶּלֶךְ, מִי בֶחָצֵר; וְהָמָן בָּא, לַחֲצַר בֵּית-הַמֶּלֶךְ הַחִיצוֹנָה, לֵאמֹר לַמֶּלֶךְ, לִתְלוֹת אֶת-מָרְדֳּכַי עַל-הָעֵץ אֲשֶׁר-הֵכִין לוֹ.

4 And the king said: 'Who is in the court?'--Now Haman was come into the outer court of the king's house, to speak unto the king to hang Mordecai on the gallows that he had prepared for him.--

ה וַיֹּאמְרוּ נַעֲרֵי הַמֶּלֶךְ, אֵלָיו--הִנֵּה הָמָן, עֹמֵד בֶּחָצֵר; וַיֹּאמֶר הַמֶּלֶךְ, יָבוֹא.

5 And the king's servants said unto him: 'Behold, Haman standeth in the court.' And the king said: 'Let him come in.'

ו וַיָּבוֹא, הָמָן, וַיֹּאמֶר לוֹ הַמֶּלֶךְ, מַה-לַעֲשׂוֹת בָּאִישׁ אֲשֶׁר הַמֶּלֶךְ חָפֵץ בִּיקָרוֹ; וַיֹּאמֶר הָמָן, בְּלִבּוֹ, לְמִי יַחְפֹּץ הַמֶּלֶךְ לַעֲשׂוֹת יְקָר, יוֹתֵר מִמֶּנִּי.

6 So Haman came in. And the king said unto him: 'What shall be done unto the man whom the king delighteth to honour?'--Now Haman said in his heart: 'Whom would the king delight to honour besides myself?'--

ז וַיֹּאמֶר הָמָן, אֶל-הַמֶּלֶךְ: אִישׁ, אֲשֶׁר הַמֶּלֶךְ חָפֵץ בִּיקָרוֹ.

7 And Haman said unto the king: 'For the man whom the king delighteth to honour,

8 let royal apparel be brought which the king useth to wear, and the horse that the king rideth upon, and on whose head a crown royal is set;

ח יָבִיאוּ לְבוּשׁ מַלְכוּת, אֲשֶׁר לָבַשׁ-בּוֹ הַמֶּלֶךְ; וְסוּס, אֲשֶׁר רָכַב עָלָיו הַמֶּלֶךְ, וַאֲשֶׁר נִתַּן כֶּתֶר מַלְכוּת, בְּרֹאשׁוֹ.

9 and let the apparel and the horse be delivered to the hand of one of the king's most noble princes, that they may array the man therewith whom the king delighteth to honour, and cause him to ride on horseback through the street of the city, and proclaim before him: Thus shall it be done to the man whom the king delighteth to honour.'

ט וְנָתוֹן הַלְּבוּשׁ וְהַסּוּס, עַל-יַד-אִישׁ מִשָּׂרֵי הַמֶּלֶךְ הַפַּרְתְּמִים, וְהִלְבִּישׁוּ אֶת-הָאִישׁ, אֲשֶׁר הַמֶּלֶךְ חָפֵץ בִּיקָרוֹ; וְהִרְכִּיבֻהוּ עַל-הַסּוּס, בִּרְחוֹב הָעִיר, וְקָרְאוּ לְפָנָיו, כָּכָה יֵעָשֶׂה לָאִישׁ אֲשֶׁר הַמֶּלֶךְ חָפֵץ בִּיקָרוֹ.

10 Then the king said to Haman: 'Make haste, and take the apparel and the horse, as thou hast said, and do even so to Mordecai the Jew, that sitteth at the king's gate; let nothing fail of all that thou hast spoken.'

י וַיֹּאמֶר הַמֶּלֶךְ לְהָמָן, מַהֵר קַח אֶת-הַלְּבוּשׁ וְאֶת-הַסּוּס כַּאֲשֶׁר דִּבַּרְתָּ, וַעֲשֵׂה-כֵן לְמָרְדֳּכַי הַיְּהוּדִי, הַיּוֹשֵׁב בְּשַׁעַר הַמֶּלֶךְ: אַל-תַּפֵּל דָּבָר, מִכֹּל אֲשֶׁר דִּבַּרְתָּ.

11 Then took Haman the apparel and the horse, and arrayed Mordecai, and caused him to ride through the street of the city, and proclaimed before him: 'Thus shall it be done unto the man whom the king delighteth to honour.'

יא וַיִּקַּח הָמָן אֶת-הַלְּבוּשׁ וְאֶת-הַסּוּס, וַיַּלְבֵּשׁ אֶת-מָרְדֳּכָי; וַיַּרְכִּיבֵהוּ, בִּרְחוֹב הָעִיר, וַיִּקְרָא לְפָנָיו, כָּכָה יֵעָשֶׂה לָאִישׁ אֲשֶׁר הַמֶּלֶךְ חָפֵץ בִּיקָרוֹ.

12 And Mordecai returned to the king's gate. But Haman hasted to his house, mourning and having his head covered.

יב וַיָּשָׁב מָרְדֳּכַי, אֶל-שַׁעַר הַמֶּלֶךְ; וְהָמָן נִדְחַף אֶל-בֵּיתוֹ, אָבֵל וַחֲפוּי רֹאשׁ.

13 And Haman recounted unto Zeresh his wife and all his friends every thing that had befallen him. Then said his wise men and Zeresh his wife unto him: 'If Mordecai, before whom thou hast begun to fall, he of the seed of the Jews, thou shalt not prevail against him, but shalt surely fall before him.'

יג וַיְסַפֵּר הָמָן לְזֶרֶשׁ אִשְׁתּוֹ, וּלְכָל-אֹהֲבָיו, אֵת, כָּל-אֲשֶׁר קָרָהוּ; וַיֹּאמְרוּ לוֹ חֲכָמָיו וְזֶרֶשׁ אִשְׁתּוֹ, אִם מִזֶּרַע הַיְּהוּדִים מָרְדֳּכַי אֲשֶׁר הַחִלּוֹתָ לִנְפֹּל לְפָנָיו לֹא-תוּכַל לוֹ--כִּי-נָפוֹל תִּפּוֹל, לְפָנָיו.

יד עוֹדָם מְדַבְּרִים עִמּוֹ,
וְסָרִיסֵי הַמֶּלֶךְ הִגִּיעוּ ;
וַיַּבְהִלוּ לְהָבִיא אֶת־
הָמָן, אֶל־הַמִּשְׁתֶּה
אֲשֶׁר־עָשְׂתָה אֶסְתֵּר.

14 While they were yet talking with him, came the king's chamberlains, and hastened to bring Haman unto the banquet that Esther had prepared.

Esther Chapter 7 אֶסְתֵּר

א וַיָּבֹא הַמֶּלֶךְ וְהָמָן, לִשְׁתּוֹת עִם-אֶסְתֵּר הַמַּלְכָּה.

1 So the king and Haman came to banquet with Esther the queen.

ב וַיֹּאמֶר הַמֶּלֶךְ לְאֶסְתֵּר גַּם בַּיּוֹם הַשֵּׁנִי, בְּמִשְׁתֵּה הַיַּיִן--מַה-שְּׁאֵלָתֵךְ אֶסְתֵּר הַמַּלְכָּה, וְתִנָּתֵן לָךְ; וּמַה-בַּקָּשָׁתֵךְ עַד-חֲצִי הַמַּלְכוּת, וְתֵעָשׂ.

2 And the king said again unto Esther on the second day at the banquet of wine: 'Whatever thy petition, queen Esther, it shall be granted thee; and whatever thy request, even to the half of the kingdom, it shall be performed.'

ג וַתַּעַן אֶסְתֵּר הַמַּלְכָּה, וַתֹּאמַר--אִם-מָצָאתִי חֵן בְּעֵינֶיךָ הַמֶּלֶךְ, וְאִם-עַל-הַמֶּלֶךְ טוֹב: תִּנָּתֶן-לִי נַפְשִׁי בִּשְׁאֵלָתִי, וְעַמִּי בְּבַקָּשָׁתִי.

3 Then Esther the queen answered and said: 'If I have found favour in thy sight, O king, and if it please the king, let my life be given me at my petition, and my people at my request;

4 for we are sold, I and my people, to be destroyed, to be slain, and to perish. But if we had been sold for bondmen and bondwomen, I had held my peace, for the adversary is not worthy that the king be endamaged.' {S}

5 Then spoke the king Ahasuerus and said unto Esther the queen: 'Who is he, and where is he, that durst presume in his heart to do so?'

6 And Esther said: 'An adversary and an enemy, even this wicked Haman.' Then Haman was terrified before the king and the queen.

ד כִּי נִמְכַּרְנוּ אֲנִי וְעַמִּי, לְהַשְׁמִיד לַהֲרוֹג וּלְאַבֵּד; וְאִלּוּ לַעֲבָדִים וְלִשְׁפָחוֹת נִמְכַּרְנוּ, הֶחֱרַשְׁתִּי--כִּי אֵין הַצָּר שֹׁוֶה, בְּנֵזֶק הַמֶּלֶךְ. {ס}

ה וַיֹּאמֶר הַמֶּלֶךְ אֲחַשְׁוֵרוֹשׁ, וַיֹּאמֶר לְאֶסְתֵּר הַמַּלְכָּה: מִי הוּא זֶה וְאֵי-זֶה הוּא, אֲשֶׁר-מְלָאוֹ לִבּוֹ לַעֲשׂוֹת כֵּן.

ו וַתֹּאמֶר אֶסְתֵּר--אִישׁ צַר וְאוֹיֵב, הָמָן הָרָע הַזֶּה; וְהָמָן נִבְעַת, מִלִּפְנֵי הַמֶּלֶךְ וְהַמַּלְכָּה.

ז וְהַמֶּלֶךְ קָם בַּחֲמָתוֹ,
מִמִּשְׁתֵּה הַיַּיִן, אֶל-גִּנַּת
הַבִּיתָן; וְהָמָן עָמַד,
לְבַקֵּשׁ עַל-נַפְשׁוֹ מֵאֶסְתֵּר
הַמַּלְכָּה--כִּי רָאָה, כִּי-
כָלְתָה אֵלָיו הָרָעָה מֵאֵת
הַמֶּלֶךְ.

ח וְהַמֶּלֶךְ שָׁב מִגִּנַּת
הַבִּיתָן אֶל-בֵּית מִשְׁתֵּה
הַיַּיִן, וְהָמָן נֹפֵל עַל-
הַמִּטָּה אֲשֶׁר אֶסְתֵּר
עָלֶיהָ, וַיֹּאמֶר הַמֶּלֶךְ,
הֲגַם לִכְבּוֹשׁ אֶת-הַמַּלְכָּה
עִמִּי בַּבָּיִת; הַדָּבָר, יָצָא
מִפִּי הַמֶּלֶךְ, וּפְנֵי הָמָן,
חָפוּ.

7 And the king arose in his wrath from the banquet of wine and went into the palace garden; but Haman remained to make request for his life to Esther the queen; for he saw that there was evil determined against him by the king.

8 Then the king returned out of the palace garden into the place of the banquet of wine; and Haman was fallen upon the couch whereon Esther was. Then said the king: 'Will he even force the queen before me in the house?' As the word went out of the king's mouth, they covered Haman's face.

9 Then said Harbonah, one of the chamberlains that were before the king: 'Behold also, the gallows fifty cubits high, which Haman hath made for Mordecai, who spoke good for the king, standeth in the house of Haman.' And the king said: 'Hang him thereon.'

ט וַיֹּאמֶר חַרְבוֹנָה אֶחָד מִן-הַסָּרִיסִים לִפְנֵי הַמֶּלֶךְ, גַּם הִנֵּה-הָעֵץ אֲשֶׁר-עָשָׂה הָמָן לְמָרְדֳּכַי אֲשֶׁר דִּבֶּר-טוֹב עַל-הַמֶּלֶךְ עֹמֵד בְּבֵית הָמָן-- גָּבֹהַּ, חֲמִשִּׁים אַמָּה; וַיֹּאמֶר הַמֶּלֶךְ, תְּלֻהוּ עָלָיו.

10 So they hanged Haman on the gallows that he had prepared for Mordecai. Then was the king's wrath assuaged. {S}

י וַיִּתְלוּ, אֶת-הָמָן, עַל-הָעֵץ, אֲשֶׁר-הֵכִין לְמָרְדֳּכָי; וַחֲמַת הַמֶּלֶךְ, שָׁכָכָה. {ס}

Esther Chapter 8 אֶסְתֵּר

א בַּיּוֹם הַהוּא, נָתַן
הַמֶּלֶךְ אֲחַשְׁוֵרוֹשׁ לְאֶסְתֵּר
הַמַּלְכָּה, אֶת-בֵּית הָמָן,
צֹרֵר היהודיים
(הַיְּהוּדִים); וּמָרְדֳּכַי, בָּא
לִפְנֵי הַמֶּלֶךְ--כִּי-הִגִּידָה
אֶסְתֵּר, מַה הוּא-לָהּ.

1 On that day did the king Ahasuerus give the house of Haman the Jews' enemy unto Esther the queen. And Mordecai came before the king; for Esther had told what he was unto her.

ב וַיָּסַר הַמֶּלֶךְ אֶת-
טַבַּעְתּוֹ, אֲשֶׁר הֶעֱבִיר
מֵהָמָן, וַיִּתְּנָהּ, לְמָרְדֳּכָי;
וַתָּשֶׂם אֶסְתֵּר אֶת-
מָרְדֳּכַי, עַל-בֵּית
הָמָן. {ס}

2 And the king took off his ring, which he had taken from Haman, and gave it unto Mordecai. And Esther set Mordecai over the house of Haman. {S}

ג וַתּוֹסֶף אֶסְתֵּר, וַתְּדַבֵּר
לִפְנֵי הַמֶּלֶךְ, וַתִּפֹּל, לִפְנֵי
רַגְלָיו; וַתֵּבְךְּ וַתִּתְחַנֶּן-לוֹ,
לְהַעֲבִיר אֶת-רָעַת הָמָן
הָאֲגָגִי, וְאֵת מַחֲשַׁבְתּוֹ,
אֲשֶׁר חָשַׁב עַל-הַיְּהוּדִים.

3 And Esther spoke yet again before the king, and fell down at his feet, and besought him with tears to put away the mischief of Haman the Agagite, and his device that he had devised against the Jews.

ד וַיּוֹשֶׁט הַמֶּלֶךְ לְאֶסְתֵּר,
אֶת שַׁרְבִט הַזָּהָב; וַתָּקָם
אֶסְתֵּר, וַתַּעֲמֹד לִפְנֵי
הַמֶּלֶךְ.

4 Then the king held out to Esther the golden sceptre. So Esther arose, and stood before the king.

ה וַתֹּאמֶר אִם-עַל-הַמֶּלֶךְ טוֹב וְאִם-מָצָאתִי חֵן לְפָנָיו, וְכָשֵׁר הַדָּבָר לִפְנֵי הַמֶּלֶךְ, וְטוֹבָה אֲנִי, בְּעֵינָיו--יִכָּתֵב לְהָשִׁיב אֶת-הַסְּפָרִים, מַחֲשֶׁבֶת הָמָן בֶּן-הַמְּדָתָא הָאֲגָגִי, אֲשֶׁר כָּתַב לְאַבֵּד אֶת-הַיְּהוּדִים, אֲשֶׁר בְּכָל-מְדִינוֹת הַמֶּלֶךְ.

5 And she said: 'If it please the king, and if I have found favour in his sight, and the thing seem right before the king, and I be pleasing in his eyes, let it be written to reverse the letters devised by Haman the son of Hammedatha the Agagite, which he wrote to destroy the Jews that are in all the king's provinces;

ו כִּי אֵיכָכָה אוּכַל, וְרָאִיתִי, בָּרָעָה, אֲשֶׁר-יִמְצָא אֶת-עַמִּי; וְאֵיכָכָה אוּכַל וְרָאִיתִי, בְּאָבְדַן מוֹלַדְתִּי. {ס}

6 for how can I endure to see the evil that shall come unto my people? or how can I endure to see the destruction of my kindred?' {S}

ז וַיֹּאמֶר הַמֶּלֶךְ אֲחַשְׁוֵרֹשׁ לְאֶסְתֵּר הַמַּלְכָּה, וּלְמָרְדֳּכַי הַיְּהוּדִי: הִנֵּה בֵית-הָמָן נָתַתִּי לְאֶסְתֵּר, וְאֹתוֹ תָּלוּ עַל-הָעֵץ--עַל אֲשֶׁר-שָׁלַח יָדוֹ, ביהודיים (בַּיְּהוּדִים).

7 Then the king Ahasuerus said unto Esther the queen and to Mordecai the Jew: 'Behold, I have given Esther the house of Haman, and him they have hanged upon the gallows, because he laid his hand upon the Jews.

ח וְאַתֶּם כִּתְבוּ עַל-
הַיְּהוּדִים כַּטּוֹב בְּעֵינֵיכֶם,
בְּשֵׁם הַמֶּלֶךְ, וְחִתְמוּ,
בְּטַבַּעַת הַמֶּלֶךְ : כִּי-כְתָב
אֲשֶׁר-נִכְתָּב בְּשֵׁם-הַמֶּלֶךְ,
וְנַחְתּוֹם בְּטַבַּעַת הַמֶּלֶךְ--
אֵין לְהָשִׁיב.

ט וַיִּקָּרְאוּ סֹפְרֵי-הַמֶּלֶךְ
בָּעֵת-הַהִיא בַּחֹדֶשׁ
הַשְּׁלִישִׁי הוּא-חֹדֶשׁ סִיוָן,
בִּשְׁלוֹשָׁה וְעֶשְׂרִים בּוֹ,
וַיִּכָּתֵב כְּכָל-אֲשֶׁר-צִוָּה
מָרְדֳּכַי אֶל-הַיְּהוּדִים וְאֶל
הָאֲחַשְׁדַּרְפְּנִים-וְהַפַּחוֹת
וְשָׂרֵי הַמְּדִינוֹת אֲשֶׁר
מֵהֹדּוּ וְעַד-כּוּשׁ שֶׁבַע
וְעֶשְׂרִים וּמֵאָה מְדִינָה,
מְדִינָה וּמְדִינָה כִּכְתָבָהּ
וְעַם וָעָם כִּלְשֹׁנוֹ ; וְאֶל-
הַיְּהוּדִים--כִּכְתָבָם,
וְכִלְשׁוֹנָם.

8 Write ye also concerning the Jews, as it liketh you, in the king's name, and seal it with the king's ring; for the writing which is written in the king's name, and sealed with the king's ring, may no man reverse.'

9 Then were the king's scribes called at that time, in the third month, which is the month Sivan, on the three and twentieth day thereof; and it was written according to all that Mordecai commanded concerning the Jews, even to the satraps, and the governors and princes of the provinces which are from India unto Ethiopia, a hundred twenty and seven provinces, unto every province according to the writing thereof, and unto every people after their language, and to thc Jews according to their writing, and according to their language.

10 And they wrote in the name of king Ahasuerus, and sealed it with the king's ring, and sent letters by posts on horseback, riding on swift steeds that were used in the king's service, bred of the stud;

י וַיִּכְתֹּב, בְּשֵׁם הַמֶּלֶךְ אֲחַשְׁוֵרֹשׁ, וַיַּחְתֹּם, בְּטַבַּעַת הַמֶּלֶךְ; וַיִּשְׁלַח סְפָרִים בְּיַד הָרָצִים בַּסּוּסִים רֹכְבֵי הָרֶכֶשׁ, הָאֲחַשְׁתְּרָנִים--בְּנֵי, הָרַמָּכִים.

11 that the king had granted the Jews that were in every city to gather themselves together, and to stand for their life, to destroy, and to slay, and to cause to perish, all the forces of the people and province that would assault them, their little ones and women, and to take the spoil of them for a prey,

יא אֲשֶׁר נָתַן הַמֶּלֶךְ לַיְּהוּדִים אֲשֶׁר בְּכָל-עִיר-וָעִיר, לְהִקָּהֵל וְלַעֲמֹד עַל-נַפְשָׁם-- לְהַשְׁמִיד וְלַהֲרֹג וּלְאַבֵּד אֶת-כָּל-חֵיל עַם וּמְדִינָה הַצָּרִים אֹתָם, טַף וְנָשִׁים; וּשְׁלָלָם, לָבוֹז.

12 upon one day in all the provinces of king Ahasuerus, namely, upon the thirteenth day of the twelfth month, which is the month Adar.

יב בְּיוֹם אֶחָד, בְּכָל-מְדִינוֹת הַמֶּלֶךְ אֲחַשְׁוֵרוֹשׁ--בִּשְׁלוֹשָׁה עָשָׂר לְחֹדֶשׁ שְׁנֵים-עָשָׂר, הוּא-חֹדֶשׁ אֲדָר.

13 The copy of the writing, to be given out for a decree in every province, was to be published unto all the peoples, and that the Jews should be ready against that day to avenge themselves on their enemies.

יג פַּתְשֶׁגֶן הַכְּתָב, לְהִנָּתֵן דָּת בְּכָל-מְדִינָה וּמְדִינָה, גָּלוּי, לְכָל-הָעַמִּים ; וְלִהְיוֹת היהודיים (הַיְּהוּדִים) עתודים (עֲתִידִים) לַיּוֹם הַזֶּה, לְהִנָּקֵם מֵאֹיְבֵיהֶם.

14 So the posts that rode upon swift steeds that were used in the king's service went out, being hastened and pressed on by the king's commandment; and the decree was given out in Shushan the castle. {S}

יד הָרָצִים רֹכְבֵי הָרֶכֶשׁ, הָאֲחַשְׁתְּרָנִים, יָצְאוּ מְבֹהָלִים וּדְחוּפִים, בִּדְבַר הַמֶּלֶךְ ; וְהַדָּת נִתְּנָה, בְּשׁוּשַׁן הַבִּירָה. {ס}

15 And Mordecai went forth from the presence of the king in royal apparel of blue and white, and with a great crown of gold, and with a robe of fine linen and purple; and the city of Shushan shouted and was glad.

טו וּמָרְדֳּכַי יָצָא מִלִּפְנֵי הַמֶּלֶךְ, בִּלְבוּשׁ מַלְכוּת תְּכֵלֶת וָחוּר, וַעֲטֶרֶת זָהָב גְּדוֹלָה, וְתַכְרִיךְ בּוּץ וְאַרְגָּמָן ; וְהָעִיר שׁוּשָׁן, צָהֲלָה וְשָׂמֵחָה.

טז לַיְּהוּדִים, הָיְתָה
אוֹרָה וְשִׂמְחָה, וְשָׂשֹׂן,
וִיקָר.

16 The Jews had light and gladness, and joy and honour.

יז וּבְכָל-מְדִינָה וּמְדִינָה
וּבְכָל-עִיר וָעִיר, מְקוֹם
אֲשֶׁר דְּבַר-הַמֶּלֶךְ וְדָתוֹ
מַגִּיעַ, שִׂמְחָה וְשָׂשֹׂן
לַיְּהוּדִים, מִשְׁתֶּה וְיוֹם
טוֹב; וְרַבִּים מֵעַמֵּי
הָאָרֶץ, מִתְיַהֲדִים--כִּי-
נָפַל פַּחַד-הַיְּהוּדִים,
עֲלֵיהֶם.

17 And in every province, and in every city, whithersoever the king's commandment and his decree came, the Jews had gladness and joy, a feast and a good day. And many from among the peoples of the land became Jews; for the fear of the Jews was fallen upon them.

Esther Chapter 9 אֶסְתֵּר

א וּבִשְׁנֵים עָשָׂר חֹדֶשׁ הוּא-חֹדֶשׁ אֲדָר, בִּשְׁלוֹשָׁה עָשָׂר יוֹם בּוֹ, אֲשֶׁר הִגִּיעַ דְּבַר-הַמֶּלֶךְ וְדָתוֹ, לְהֵעָשׂוֹת: בַּיּוֹם, אֲשֶׁר שִׂבְּרוּ אֹיְבֵי הַיְּהוּדִים לִשְׁלוֹט בָּהֶם, וְנַהֲפוֹךְ הוּא, אֲשֶׁר יִשְׁלְטוּ הַיְּהוּדִים הֵמָּה בְּשֹׂנְאֵיהֶם.

1 Now in the twelfth month, which is the month Adar, on the thirteenth day of the same, when the king's commandment and his decree drew near to be put in execution, in the day that the enemies of the Jews hoped to have rule over them; whereas it was turned to the contrary, that the Jews had rule over them that hated them;

ב נִקְהֲלוּ הַיְּהוּדִים בְּעָרֵיהֶם, בְּכָל-מְדִינוֹת הַמֶּלֶךְ אֲחַשְׁוֵרוֹשׁ, לִשְׁלֹחַ יָד, בִּמְבַקְשֵׁי רָעָתָם; וְאִישׁ לֹא-עָמַד לִפְנֵיהֶם, כִּי-נָפַל פַּחְדָּם עַל-כָּל-הָעַמִּים.

2 the Jews gathered themselves together in their cities throughout all the provinces of the king Ahasuerus, to lay hand on such as sought their hurt; and no man could withstand them; for the fear of them was fallen upon all the peoples.

ג וְכָל-שָׂרֵי הַמְּדִינוֹת וְהָאֲחַשְׁדַּרְפְּנִים וְהַפַּחוֹת, וְעֹשֵׂי הַמְּלָאכָה אֲשֶׁר לַמֶּלֶךְ--מְנַשְּׂאִים, אֶת-הַיְּהוּדִים: כִּי-נָפַל פַּחַד-מָרְדֳּכַי, עֲלֵיהֶם.

3 And all the princes of the provinces, and the satraps, and the governors, and they that did the king's business, helped the Jews; because the fear of Mordecai was fallen upon them.

4 For Mordecai was great in the king's house, and his fame went forth throughout all the provinces; for the man Mordecai waxed greater and greater.

ד כִּי-גָדוֹל מָרְדֳּכַי בְּבֵית הַמֶּלֶךְ, וְשָׁמְעוֹ הוֹלֵךְ בְּכָל-הַמְּדִינוֹת: כִּי-הָאִישׁ מָרְדֳּכַי, הוֹלֵךְ וְגָדוֹל.

5 And the Jews smote all their enemies with the stroke of the sword, and with slaughter and destruction, and did what they would unto them that hated them.

ה וַיַּכּוּ הַיְּהוּדִים בְּכָל-אֹיְבֵיהֶם, מַכַּת-חֶרֶב וְהֶרֶג וְאַבְדָן; וַיַּעֲשׂוּ בְשֹׂנְאֵיהֶם, כִּרְצוֹנָם.

6 And in Shushan the castle the Jews slew and destroyed five hundred men. {S}

ו וּבְשׁוּשַׁן הַבִּירָה, הָרְגוּ הַיְּהוּדִים וְאַבֵּד--חֲמֵשׁ מֵאוֹת, {ר} אִישׁ. {ס}

7 And {S} Parshandatha, and {S} Dalphon, and {S} Aspatha,

ז וְאֵת {ר} פַּרְשַׁנְדָּ**תָ** א {ס} וְאֵת {ר} דַּלְ פוֹן, {ס} וְאֵת {ר} אַסְפָּתָא. {ס}

8 and {S} Poratha, and {S} Adalia, and {S} Aridatha,

ח וְאֵת {ר} פּוֹרָתָא {ס} וְאֵת {ר} אֲדַלְיָ א, {ס} וְאֵת {ר} אֲ רִידָתָא. {ס}

ט וְאֵת {ר} פַּרְמַשְׁתָּ
א {ס} וְאֵת {ר} אֲרִי
סַי, {ס} וְאֵת {ר} אֲ
רִידַי {ס} וְאֵת {ר} וַ
יְזָתָא. {ס}

9 and {S} Parmashta, and {S} Arisai, and {S} Aridai, and {S} Vaizatha, {S}

י עֲשֶׂרֶת {ר} בְּנֵי הָמָן
בֶּן־הַמְּדָתָא, צֹרֵר
הַיְּהוּדִים--הָרָגוּ;
וּבַבִּזָּה--לֹא שָׁלְחוּ, אֶת־
יָדָם.

10 the ten sons of Haman the son of Hammedatha, the Jews' enemy, slew they; but on the spoil they laid not their hand.

יא בַּיּוֹם הַהוּא, בָּא
מִסְפַּר הַהֲרוּגִים בְּשׁוּשַׁן
הַבִּירָה--לִפְנֵי הַמֶּלֶךְ.

11 On that day the number of those that were slain in Shushan the castle was brought before the king.

יב וַיֹּאמֶר הַמֶּלֶךְ
לְאֶסְתֵּר הַמַּלְכָּה,
בְּשׁוּשַׁן הַבִּירָה הָרְגוּ
הַיְּהוּדִים וְאַבֵּד חֲמֵשׁ
מֵאוֹת אִישׁ וְאֵת עֲשֶׂרֶת
בְּנֵי־הָמָן--בִּשְׁאָר
מְדִינוֹת הַמֶּלֶךְ, מֶה
עָשׂוּ; וּמַה־שְּׁאֵלָתֵךְ
וְיִנָּתֵן לָךְ, וּמַה־בַּקָּשָׁתֵךְ
עוֹד וְתֵעָשׂ.

12 And the king said unto Esther the queen: 'The Jews have slain and destroyed five hundred men in Shushan the castle, and the ten sons of Haman; what then have they done in the rest of the king's provinces! Now whatever thy petition, it shall be granted thee; and whatever thy request further, it shall be done.'

13 Then said Esther: 'If it please the king, let it be granted to the Jews that are in Shushan to do to-morrow also according unto this day's decree, and let Haman's ten sons be hanged upon the gallows.'

יג וַתֹּאמֶר אֶסְתֵּר, אִם-עַל-הַמֶּלֶךְ טוֹב-- יִנָּתֵן גַּם-מָחָר לַיְּהוּדִים אֲשֶׁר בְּשׁוּשָׁן, לַעֲשׂוֹת כְּדָת הַיּוֹם ; וְאֵת עֲשֶׂרֶת בְּנֵי-הָמָן, יִתְלוּ עַל-הָעֵץ .

14 And the king commanded it so to be done; and a decree was given out in Shushan; and they hanged Haman's ten sons.

יד וַיֹּאמֶר הַמֶּלֶךְ לְהֵעָשׂוֹת כֵּן, וַתִּנָּתֵן דָּת בְּשׁוּשָׁן ; וְאֵת עֲשֶׂרֶת בְּנֵי-הָמָן, תָּלוּ.

15 And the Jews that were in Shushan gathered themselves together on the fourteenth day also of the month Adar, and slew three hundred men in Shushan; but on the spoil they laid not their hand.

טו וַיִּקָּהֲלוּ היהודיים (הַיְּהוּדִים) אֲשֶׁר-בְּשׁוּשָׁן, גַּם בְּיוֹם אַרְבָּעָה עָשָׂר לְחֹדֶשׁ אֲדָר, וַיַּהַרְגוּ בְשׁוּשָׁן, שְׁלֹשׁ מֵאוֹת אִישׁ ; וּבַבִּזָּה--לֹא שָׁלְחוּ, אֶת-יָדָם.

טז וּשְׁאָר הַיְּהוּדִים אֲשֶׁר בִּמְדִינוֹת הַמֶּלֶךְ נִקְהֲלוּ וְעָמֹד עַל-נַפְשָׁם, וְנוֹחַ מֵאֹיְבֵיהֶם, וְהָרוֹג בְּשֹׂנְאֵיהֶם, חֲמִשָּׁה וְשִׁבְעִים אָלֶף ; וּבַבִּזָּה-- לֹא שָׁלְחוּ, אֶת-יָדָם.

16 And the other Jews that were in the king's provinces gathered themselves together, and stood for their lives, and had rest from their enemies, and slew of them that hated them seventy and five thousand--but on the spoil they laid not their hand--

יז בְּיוֹם-שְׁלוֹשָׁה עָשָׂר, לְחֹדֶשׁ אֲדָר ; וְנוֹחַ, בְּאַרְבָּעָה עָשָׂר בּוֹ, וְעָשֹׂה אֹתוֹ, יוֹם מִשְׁתֶּה וְשִׂמְחָה.

17 on the thirteenth day of the month Adar, and on the fourteenth day of the same they rested, and made it a day of feasting and gladness.

יח והיהודיים (וְהַיְּהוּדִים) אֲשֶׁר-בְּשׁוּשָׁן, נִקְהֲלוּ בִּשְׁלוֹשָׁה עָשָׂר בּוֹ, וּבְאַרְבָּעָה עָשָׂר, בּוֹ ; וְנוֹחַ, בַּחֲמִשָּׁה עָשָׂר בּוֹ, וְעָשֹׂה אֹתוֹ, יוֹם מִשְׁתֶּה וְשִׂמְחָה.

18 But the Jews that were in Shushan assembled together on the thirteenth day thereof, and on the fourteenth thereof; and on the fifteenth day of the same they rested, and made it a day of feasting and gladness.

19 Therefore do the Jews of the villages, that dwell in the unwalled towns, make the fourteenth day of the month Adar a day of gladness and feasting, and a good day, and of sending portions one to another.

יט עַל-כֵּן הַיְּהוּדִים הַפְּרוֹזִים (הַפְּרָזִים), הַיֹּשְׁבִים בְּעָרֵי הַפְּרָזוֹת--עֹשִׂים אֵת יוֹם אַרְבָּעָה עָשָׂר לְחֹדֶשׁ אֲדָר, שִׂמְחָה וּמִשְׁתֶּה וְיוֹם טוֹב; וּמִשְׁלֹחַ מָנוֹת, אִישׁ לְרֵעֵהוּ.

20 And Mordecai wrote these things, and sent letters unto all the Jews that were in all the provinces of the king Ahasuerus, both nigh and far,

כ וַיִּכְתֹּב מָרְדֳּכַי, אֶת-הַדְּבָרִים הָאֵלֶּה; וַיִּשְׁלַח סְפָרִים אֶל-כָּל-הַיְּהוּדִים, אֲשֶׁר בְּכָל-מְדִינוֹת הַמֶּלֶךְ אֲחַשְׁוֵרוֹשׁ--הַקְּרוֹבִים, וְהָרְחוֹקִים.

21 to enjoin them that they should keep the fourteenth day of the month Adar, and the fifteenth day of the same, yearly,

כא לְקַיֵּם, עֲלֵיהֶם--לִהְיוֹת עֹשִׂים אֵת יוֹם אַרְבָּעָה עָשָׂר לְחֹדֶשׁ אֲדָר, וְאֵת יוֹם-חֲמִשָּׁה עָשָׂר בּוֹ : בְּכָל-שָׁנָה, וְשָׁנָה.

כב כַּיָּמִים, אֲשֶׁר-נָחוּ בָהֶם הַיְּהוּדִים מֵאוֹיְבֵיהֶם, וְהַחֹדֶשׁ אֲשֶׁר נֶהְפַּךְ לָהֶם מִיָּגוֹן לְשִׂמְחָה, וּמֵאֵבֶל לְיוֹם טוֹב; לַעֲשׂוֹת אוֹתָם, יְמֵי מִשְׁתֶּה וְשִׂמְחָה, וּמִשְׁלֹחַ מָנוֹת אִישׁ לְרֵעֵהוּ, וּמַתָּנוֹת לָאֶבְיוֹנִים.

22 the days wherein the Jews had rest from their enemies, and the month which turned unto them from sorrow to gladness, and from mourning into a good day; that they should make them days of feasting and gladness, and of sending portions one to another, and gifts to the poor.

כג וְקִבֵּל, הַיְּהוּדִים, אֵת אֲשֶׁר-הֵחֵלּוּ, לַעֲשׂוֹת; וְאֵת אֲשֶׁר-כָּתַב מָרְדֳּכַי, אֲלֵיהֶם.

23 And the Jews took upon them to do as they had begun, and as Mordecai had written unto them;

כד כִּי הָמָן בֶּן-הַמְּדָתָא הָאֲגָגִי, צֹרֵר כָּל-הַיְּהוּדִים--חָשַׁב עַל-הַיְּהוּדִים, לְאַבְּדָם; וְהִפִּל פּוּר הוּא הַגּוֹרָל, לְהֻמָּם וּלְאַבְּדָם.

24 because Haman the son of Hammedatha, the Agagite, the enemy of all the Jews, had devised against the Jews to destroy them, and had cast pur, that is, the lot, to discomfit them, and to destroy them;

כה וּבְבֹאָהּ, לִפְנֵי הַמֶּלֶךְ, אָמַר עִם-הַסֵּפֶר, יָשׁוּב מַחֲשַׁבְתּוֹ הָרָעָה אֲשֶׁר-חָשַׁב עַל-הַיְּהוּדִים עַל-רֹאשׁוֹ ; וְתָלוּ אֹתוֹ וְאֶת-בָּנָיו, עַל-הָעֵץ.

25 but when she came before the king, he commanded by letters that his wicked device, which he had devised against the Jews, should return upon his own head; and that he and his sons should be hanged on the gallows.

כו עַל-כֵּן קָרְאוּ לַיָּמִים הָאֵלֶּה פוּרִים, עַל-שֵׁם הַפּוּר--עַל-כֵּן, עַל-כָּל-דִּבְרֵי הָאִגֶּרֶת הַזֹּאת ; וּמָה-רָאוּ עַל-כָּכָה, וּמָה הִגִּיעַ אֲלֵיהֶם.

26 Wherefore they called these days Purim, after the name of pur. Therefore because of all the words of this letter, and of that which they had seen concerning this matter, and that which had come unto them,

כז קִיְּמוּ וקבל (וְקִבְּלוּ) הַיְּהוּדִים עֲלֵיהֶם וְעַל-זַרְעָם וְעַל כָּל-הַנִּלְוִים עֲלֵיהֶם, וְלֹא יַעֲבוֹר--לִהְיוֹת עֹשִׂים אֵת שְׁנֵי הַיָּמִים הָאֵלֶּה, כִּכְתָבָם וְכִזְמַנָּם : בְּכָל-שָׁנָה, וְשָׁנָה.

27 the Jews ordained, and took upon them, and upon their seed, and upon all such as joined themselves unto them, so as it should not fail, that they would keep these two days according to the writing thereof, and according to the appointed time thereof, every year;

28 and that these days should be remembered and kept throughout every generation, every family, every province, and every city; and that these days of Purim should not fail from among the Jews, nor the memorial of them perish from their seed. {S}

29 Then Esther the queen, the daughter of Abihail, and Mordecai the Jew, wrote down all the acts of power, to confirm this second letter of Purim.

30 And he sent letters unto all the Jews, to the hundred twenty and seven provinces of the kingdom of Ahasuerus, with words of peace and truth,

כח וְהַיָּמִים הָאֵלֶּה נִזְכָּרִים וְנַעֲשִׂים בְּכָל-דּוֹר וָדוֹר, מִשְׁפָּחָה וּמִשְׁפָּחָה, מְדִינָה וּמְדִינָה, וְעִיר וָעִיר; וִימֵי הַפּוּרִים הָאֵלֶּה, לֹא יַעַבְרוּ מִתּוֹךְ הַיְּהוּדִים, וְזִכְרָם, לֹא-יָסוּף מִזַּרְעָם. {ס}

כט וַתִּכְתֹּב אֶסְתֵּר הַמַּלְכָּה בַת-אֲבִיחַיִל, וּמָרְדֳּכַי הַיְּהוּדִי--אֶת-כָּל-תֹּקֶף: לְקַיֵּם, אֵת אִגֶּרֶת הַפֻּרִים הַזֹּאת--הַשֵּׁנִית.

ל וַיִּשְׁלַח סְפָרִים אֶל-כָּל-הַיְּהוּדִים, אֶל-שֶׁבַע וְעֶשְׂרִים וּמֵאָה מְדִינָה--מַלְכוּת, אֲחַשְׁוֵרוֹשׁ: דִּבְרֵי שָׁלוֹם, וֶאֱמֶת.

לא לְקַיֵּם אֶת-יְמֵי
הַפֻּרִים הָאֵלֶּה
בִּזְמַנֵּיהֶם, כַּאֲשֶׁר קִיַּם
עֲלֵיהֶם מָרְדֳּכַי הַיְּהוּדִי
וְאֶסְתֵּר הַמַּלְכָּה,
וְכַאֲשֶׁר קִיְּמוּ עַל-
נַפְשָׁם, וְעַל-
זַרְעָם : דִּבְרֵי הַצּוֹמוֹת,
וְזַעֲקָתָם.

31 to confirm these days of Purim in their appointed times, according as Mordecai the Jew and Esther the queen had enjoined them, and as they had ordained for themselves and for their seed, the matters of the fastings and their cry.

לב וּמַאֲמַר אֶסְתֵּר--
קִיַּם, דִּבְרֵי הַפֻּרִים
הָאֵלֶּה ; וְנִכְתָּב,
בַּסֵּפֶר. {ס}

32 And the commandment of Esther confirmed these matters of Purim; and it was written in the book. {S}

Esther Chapter 10 אֶסְתֵּר

א וַיָּשֶׂם הַמֶּלֶךְ אֲחַשְׁרֹשׁ (אֲחַשְׁוֵרוֹשׁ) מַס עַל-הָאָרֶץ, וְאִיֵּי הַיָּם.

1 And the king Ahasuerus laid a tribute upon the land, and upon the isles of the sea.

ב וְכָל-מַעֲשֵׂה תָקְפּוֹ, וּגְבוּרָתוֹ, וּפָרָשַׁת גְּדֻלַּת מָרְדֳּכַי, אֲשֶׁר גִּדְּלוֹ הַמֶּלֶךְ—הֲלוֹא-הֵם כְּתוּבִים, עַל-סֵפֶר דִּבְרֵי הַיָּמִים, לְמַלְכֵי, מָדַי וּפָרָס.

2 And all the acts of his power and of his might, and the full account of the greatness of Mordecai, how the king advanced him, are they not written in the book of the chronicles of the kings of Media and Persia?

ג כִּי מָרְדֳּכַי הַיְּהוּדִי, מִשְׁנֶה לַמֶּלֶךְ אֲחַשְׁוֵרוֹשׁ, וְגָדוֹל לַיְּהוּדִים, וְרָצוּי לְרֹב אֶחָיו—דֹּרֵשׁ טוֹב לְעַמּוֹ, וְדֹבֵר שָׁלוֹם לְכָל-זַרְעוֹ. {ש}

3 For Mordecai the Jew was next unto king Ahasuerus, and great among the Jews, and accepted of the multitude of his brethren; seeking the good of his people and speaking peace to all his seed. {P}

**THE END of this book but
Not the end of this journey**

ABOUT THE AUTHOR

ADDITIONAL BOOKS:

Poetically Correct *From* Ground To Glory

Blessed With Less

The Weak STRONG Man (The Life of Samson)

To Nineveh or Not (The Book of Jonah

**Nebuchadnezzar's Nightmares
(Daniel Chapters 2 & 4)**

The In-Love In-Laws (The Book of Ruth)

(*You Are The*) "HELP IN CRISIS"

PARKERS POETIC PUZZLES – VOL. I

http://www.ParkersPoetryPlus.com

Email: ThePoetJoel@gmail.com

IG: PoeticWitnessWear

Other Items/Works Available:

POETIC WITNESS WEAR {Imprinted Garments}
Combination of: Silk Screen, Embroidered & Cad-Cut

T-Shirts, Sweat-Shirts

Caps, Hats

Custom Jackets: wool/Leather, Nylon, Denim}

Laser Engraving

http://www.PoeticWitnessWear.com

http://www.ParkersPoetryPlus.com

Creator/Inventor of the **"HOLY GHOST MIRROR"**

http://www.HolyGhostMirror.com

Email: HolyGhostMirror.com

Let me add, many other works can be witnessed and personally experienced at:

Morning Star Highway Church of Christ
869 Halsey Street {corner of Saratoga Ave}
Brooklyn, NY 11233

Made in the USA
Middletown, DE
30 September 2021

48593189R00060